RACE RELATIONS

The Struggle for Equality in America

Barbara Diggs
Illustrated by Richard Chapman

Titles in the Inquire & Investigate
Social Issues of the Twentieth Century set

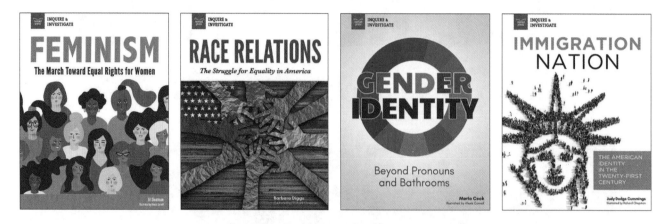

Check out more titles at www.nomadpress.net

Nomad Press
A division of Nomad Communications
10 9 8 7 6 5 4 3 2 1

This book was manufactured by Versa Press,
East Peoria, Illinois
April 2019, Job #J18-13166

ISBN Softcover: 978-1-61930-555-7
ISBN Hardcover: 978-1-61930-552-6

Educational Consultant, Marla Conn

Questions regarding the ordering of this book should be addressed to
Nomad Press
2456 Christian St.
White River Junction, VT 05001
www.nomadpress.net

FOREWORD

Race has roiled America since the country's birth more than four centuries ago. It is a dynamic force—one that has been wielded by those in power across the political and social spectrum to assign burdens and benefits, justify behavior and treatment, and determine the nature of relationships between all people. Race shapes institutions, informs decisions, and drives the policies and laws that determine the trajectories of countless lives. Simply put, it is impossible to overstate the importance of race, or the central role it plays in America. It is woven into the country's DNA.

Despite the centrality of race to American life, the ways in which it has been weaponized to produce inequality and injustice have engendered deep embarrassment and shame. These feelings are understandable. The idea that one's skin color could determine one's lot in life is dramatically out of step with the lofty ideals that rest at the heart the Constitution and the Declaration of Independence. Unfortunately, however, these feelings stunt thoughtful reflection on how the racial dynamics of the past have shaped the present and yield complex challenges for our collective future. Today, it is convenient to downplay or ignore the effects of race. Yet if we ever hope to overcome America's original sin, and to craft a future that produces equality, liberty, and justice for all, we must engage in the difficult work of honestly and unflinchingly confronting our racialized past and present.

Race Relations takes on that challenge in an accessible and thoughtful manner—one that young people can understand. By examining the history of race in America, this volume teaches young readers how race was constructed, how it determined the distribution of power, and how its lasting influence is felt today. The text, key questions, and Inquire & Investigate segments force young readers to interrogate the meaning of race throughout history. They also stimulate the type of critical, nuanced thinking rarely associated with fleeting conversations on race that so often produce more heat than light.

Notably, *Race Relations* examines race through the lens of the African American experience, while incorporating perspectives across the racial mosaic that comprises the American body politic. This approach provides readers with insights about race that have broad applicability to all people. It views history through a racial lens that is often ignored. It helps young people understand the work and sacrifice needed to chart a positive path forward. And it teaches them that the story of race in America is marked by peaks of progress and valleys of despair, buoyed by a resilience rooted in the reasonable hope and understanding that the ongoing struggle to perfect the American union must be grounded in an honest, comprehensive reckoning with the role race plays in American society. *Race Relations* accomplishes all of this for young people—the same young people who embody the hope that America will, someday, own up to its history and chart a positive path into the future.

—Vincent Southerland,
Executive Director, The Center on Race,
Inequality and the Law, New York University

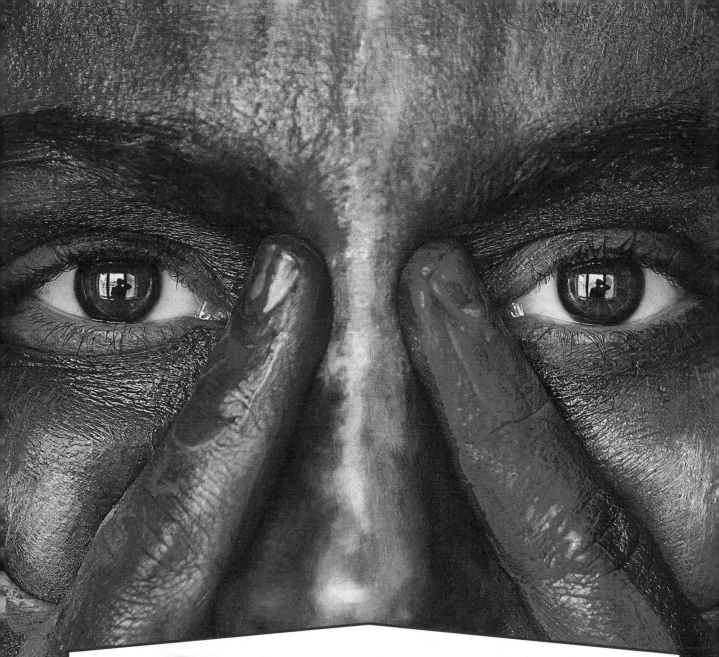

You can use a smartphone or tablet app to scan the QR codes and explore more! Cover up neighboring QR codes to make sure you're scanning the right one. You can find a list of URLs on the Resources page.

If the QR code doesn't work, try searching the internet with the Keyword Prompts to find other helpful sources.

 race relations

Interested in primary sources?
Look for this icon.

What are source notes?

In this book, you'll find small numbers at the end of some paragraphs. These numbers indicate that you can find source notes for that section in the back of the book. Source notes tell readers where the writer found their information. This might be a news article, a book, or another kind of media. Source notes are a way to know that what you are reading is information that other people have verified. They can also lead you to more places where you can explore a topic that you're curious about!

Contents

TIMELINE

1460s .... The Portuguese begin selling enslaved Africans to other Europeans.

1619 .... Approximately 20 Africans are brought to Jamestown, Virginia, on an English warship. These are the first recorded Africans in North America.

1660s .... The colonies begin passing laws to create legal and societal distinctions between Africans, Native Americans, and Europeans.

1712 .... The first revolt of enslaved people occurs in Manhattan, New York.

1777 .... General George Washington allows African Americans to fight in the American Revolution. Vermont becomes the first state to abolish slavery, and several other Northern states follow.

1790s .... An early version of the Underground Railroad begins to form.

1847 .... Chinese immigrants begin to arrive in the United States.

April 1861 .... The Civil War begins.

1863 .... U.S. President Abraham Lincoln issues the Emancipation Proclamation, declaring enslaved people in the rebelling states free.

December 1865 .... The U.S. Congress ratifies the Thirteenth Amendment to the Constitution, officially abolishing slavery.

1866 .... The Ku Klux Klan forms in the South and racial violence against African Americans becomes widespread.

1867 .... African American men vote in the South for the first time under the protection of federal military troops.

1924 .... Congress passes the Native American Act, granting citizenship to all Native Americans born in the United States.

1942 .... The United States enters World War II. The government forces Japanese Americans to relocate to internment camps. Americans of all races fight in the war.

TIMELINE

1954................................ The U.S. Supreme Court rules in *Brown v. Board of Education* that racial segregation in public schools is unconstitutional.

1955................................ Emmitt Till is murdered by white supremacists. Rosa Parks refuses to give up her seat on a bus to a white man. The Montgomery, Alabama, bus boycott begins a larger civil rights movement.

1964................................ Congress passes the Civil Rights Act of 1964 outlawing discrimination based on race, gender, religion, color, or national origin.

1968................................ Martin Luther King Jr. is assassinated. The civil rights movement wanes.

1986................................ Congress passes the Anti-Drug Abuse Act, leading to a rapid rise in the number of incarcerated African Americans.

2009................................ Barack Obama becomes the first African American president of the United States.

2012................................ Trayvon Martin, an unarmed African American teen, is shot and killed by George Zimmerman, sparking a public outcry.

2013................................ The Black Lives Matter movement forms. Several high-profile police shootings of unarmed African Americans raise numerous protests.

2015................................ A drug epidemic involving opioids and heroin helps trigger a rise in the death rates of working-class white Americans. The number of hate crimes rise.

2016................................ African American NFL football player Colin Kaepernick begins to kneel during the national anthem to protest police brutality, provoking a divisive national discussion.

2016................................ Donald Trump is elected president of the United States.

2017................................ Americans become further divided over whether to remove Confederate statues from public spaces.

2018................................ A poll shows that most Americans do not have a positive view of race relations.

Introduction ▷
Where We Now Stand

What are race relations?

Race relations are the relationships between members of different races in a country or community. While harmonious race relations exist in many neighborhoods, social communities, towns, and cities across America today, the United States has had deeply troubled race relations throughout its 400-year history.

On the evening of November 4, 2008, President-elect Barack Obama (1961–) stepped onto a stage in Grant Park, Chicago, Illinois, and waved to a jubilant crowd of more than 200,000. In the park and all over the country, millions of people danced, cheered, and even wept with joy. Even those who hadn't voted for him knew that they were living witnesses to one of the most extraordinary events in American history—an African American had just been elected president of the United States.

Just 150 years before this election, a white person could legally own, purchase, or sell a man who looked like Barack Obama, the same way they could buy and sell a horse or a wagon. One hundred years earlier, Obama might have been terrorized, beaten, or even killed if he so much as tried to register to vote. And a scant 50 years before his victory, Obama's brown skin would have gotten him booted from certain restaurants, hotels, or other establishments in some of the very states that he won.

Despite this intense culture of racism, Americans, a majority of them white, voted for Obama to hold the United States' highest office.

Many people joyfully hailed Obama's election as a sign that the country was entering a "post-racial" era, a period when racial prejudice and discrimination no longer existed. What better proof of the American Dream than the election of an African American man to the presidency?

Days after the election, a Gallup poll showed that 67 percent of Americans believed that a solution between blacks and whites "will eventually be worked out." This was the highest value Gallup had ever measured on this question.

Barack Obama is sworn in as the 44th president of the United States on January 20, 2009.

credit: Master Sgt. Cecilio Ricardo, U.S. Air Force

The same poll showed that 70 percent of Americans believed that Obama's election would make race relations better or even a lot better.[1] However, such optimism was premature.

By the end of Obama's second term, Americans were in more despair about race relations than ever. Blacks and whites were fiercely and rancorously divided over a slew of high-profile issues, from police brutality to the correct ways of protesting social injustice.

Polls showed that Latinos, too, felt race relations were deteriorating. And some Asian Americans observed with frustration that anti-Asian discrimination and sentiment got ignored altogether.

Three months after Obama left office in 2017, Gallup poll results showed that Americans' worries about race relations had reached a record high for the new millennium, displaying a level of concern that hadn't been seen since the 1950s and 1960s. A different poll done that same month revealed that 63 percent of those interviewed saw prejudice and hatred increasing in the United States.[2]

What happened?
How did the country's perception of race relations plunge so sharply from hopeful to despairing? And why are race relations in America so troubled in the first place?

The answer lies in the history of the United States. Much of the mistrust, fear, suspicion, incomprehension, anger, and hatred that can exist between people of different races today flow directly from the catastrophic way U.S. race relations began.

THE BEGINNING OF RACE RELATIONS

It's no secret that race relations in the United States began on the worst possible footing. From almost the first moment Europeans arrived in the land that would become America, they constructed a racial hierarchy to justify the enslavement and oppression of races they deemed to be inferior. European colonists did this in order to develop the land and grow rich. Needless to say, interracial relations did not flourish after that.

> It might be hard to imagine, but the concept of race was new at the time.

Prior to the fifteenth century, there was no such thing as racial categories. Africans were "Malian" or "Ethiopian," for example, not collectively "blacks." Europeans were "English" or "French," not "whites."

As Europeans increasingly traveled the world during the 1400s and 1500s, however, they more frequently encountered different people and cultures they'd had only limited or no exposure to previously. They began to broadly categorize people according to common physical characteristics, such as skin color, and a loosely shared culture. And slowly, the idea of racial categories began to take shape.

While it is a normal impulse to categorize to make sense of the unfamiliar, racial categories were formed with deeply prejudiced viewpoints and self-serving motivations. The European establishment thought its way of life and physical appearance was superior to people with darker skin or with a very different culture.

WHERE COLOR COMES FROM

Did you know that, genetically, all humans are 99.9 percent the same? Our differences in skin color are a result of small evolutionary adjustments. Human life originated in Africa, and dark pigmentation in the skin, called melanin, existed to help protect our earliest ancestors from the strength of the African sun. As people migrated to less sunny climates, melanin amounts slowly dwindled. Scientists say this change occurred because lower amounts of melanin allowed people who weren't exposed to much sunlight to better synthesize vitamin D.

Watch a video on how skin color is a product of adaptation across many, many generations at this website.

science of skin color

If these views had remained a mere preference for their own culture, the world might be a different place. But the development of these ideas of race coincided with the rise of European colonization and the growth of transatlantic African slavery. European "superiority" quickly became an excuse for European nations to enslave, dominate, and exploit people who were unlike themselves for financial gain and increased world power.

The Transatlantic Slave Trade was the process of capturing and shipping millions of men, women, and children from Africa to the United States. Many of them died on the way in ships like the one diagrammed below.

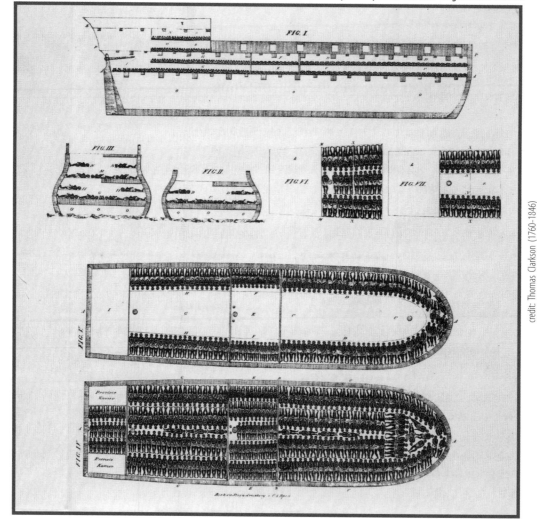

credit: Thomas Clarkson (1760–1846)

When the British created the colonies in North America in the early seventeenth century, they established laws and a culture that embraced extreme racial inequality. The laws and culture fostered the concept of European, or white, supremacy. Through racist laws, behavior, and the repetition of pejorative narratives about other races, the false perception that whites were superior to all other races, particularly blacks, became deeply ingrained in the fabric of American society.

Since then, Americans of all races have worked hard as centuries passed to change the racial inequalities built into America's laws and society. Although the most outrageous racist laws were eradicated, the unwritten racial hierarchy established so long ago can still be found in today's world in different ways.

Racial inequality continues to be present in society. It is there in the age-old racial stereotypes, prejudices, and biases that still negatively influence how different races view and act toward each other today—whether we are aware of it or not.

WHAT IS RACISM?

The fact of racism hangs over nearly every discussion about race relations. The Merriam-Webster dictionary defines racism as "a belief that race is the primary determinant of human traits and capacities and that racial differences produce an inherent superiority of a particular race."

> In other words, racism is when people believe that there is something specific to their genetic heritage that makes them superior to people with a different genetic heritage.

RACE REALITY

In the lead up to the American Civil War, the states were either slave states or free states, though all benefited economically from the institution of slavery. Take a look at this interactive map that shows the timeline of how the nation became divided by the issue of slavery. Why do you think some states chose slavery while others chose emancipation?

🔍 Learner biography America

What do you think race relations in the United States would be like if slavery hadn't been such an integral part of the country's history?

Race is a term that has no single definition. Generally speaking, race is a classification that separates people into broad categories based on observable physical characteristics, ancestry, and cultural identity. People often debate whether race is a biological or social construct. However, the majority of scientists agree that while people of a certain "race" may share some genetic commonalities, the genetic lines between different races are so blurry as to be virtually meaningless. So far, no one has found a single biological trait that is exclusive to only one race. This is why most scientists say that race is not a reliable way of classifying humans and that race is a social construct. Why might people continue to use race as a system of classification?

Racism can take a variety of forms, from overt to implicit to systemic to internalized. It's a term that's widely misunderstood and misused. People often use the word "racism" interchangeably with words that describe other harmful attitudes, such as "prejudice," "bias," and "stereotyping."

A person of any race can feel prejudice or bias toward any other person. Anyone can believe that another person will behave in a certain way simply because of some aspect of their person, whether it's their sexuality, gender, hair color, or something else. Sometimes, these biases and prejudices are based on race, even if the person with the bias doesn't consciously believe that one race is superior to another. While these thoughts or attitudes can be held without any animosity toward the group in question, they can still be tremendously harmful because they support and continue the narratives that give rise to racism.

There's serious disagreement along racial lines on the extent and degree to which racism, discrimination, and bias exist.

A 2017 CNN poll showed that 87 percent of African Americans polled say that black people face a lot of discrimination in the United States, whereas only 49 percent of white people questioned said the same. A Quinnipiac poll taken that same year showed that 66 percent of people of color say that racial prejudice in the United States is a very serious issue, but just 39 percent of whites agreed. Who is right?[3]

This large gap in even the perception of racial issues is also likely responsible for some of the racial tensions in America today. If people of different colors can't agree on the problem, how can they work to solve it?

UNDERSTANDING RACE RELATIONS

The United States' history of race relations is a painful one, full of uncomfortable inconsistencies and unpleasant truths. Although the topic is sensitive, it's important to face this difficult past with courage and persistence. This history is the key to understanding today's racial climate and continuing to work toward a more harmonious future.

Race Relations helps put the complexity of contemporary U.S. race relations into historical context. It traces the evolution of the concept of race and race relations from their beginnings in the fifteenth century through the slavery and Reconstruction periods, the Jim Crow and civil rights eras, and the presidencies of Barack Obama and Donald Trump.

Along the way, you'll meet a range of people—some famous figures, some ordinary citizens—who took great risks to fight for freedom, equality, and social justice. You'll also meet those who did their best to keep the racial hierarchy in place.

While this book primarily focuses on the changing relationship between African Americans and Americans of European descent, it also explores the historical experience of other people of color in the United States, particularly Native Americans, Latinos, and Asian Americans. We'll also look at the concerns about race held by modern Americans.

No matter your racial heritage, *Race Relations* will help you think critically and creatively about your position and role in society and gain a broader understanding of American society.

KEY QUESTIONS

- Why do you think there's such a large gap in how people of color and white people view racial issues?

- Are there any benefits to dividing people into racial categories? If so, what are they?

- If you could ask anything of a person of another race, what would it be?

Write down what you think each word means. What root words can you find to help you? What does the context of the word tell you?

bias, **discrimination**, **enslave**, **oppression**, **optimism**, **race**, **racism**, and **social construct**.

Compare your definitions with those of your friends or classmates. Did you all come up with the same meanings? Turn to the text and glossary if you need help.

To investigate more, give yourself an assignment of reading, watching, or listening to books, movies, and music produced by people from each of the different races. Does this change your perception? If so, how?

CHECK YOURSELF

History isn't the only factor that can influence our perception of races different from our own. Naturally, having a personal relationship with people of a different race plays a huge role in your perceptions, as does the nature of that relationship with them. But we also receive input from a variety of other sources— our family, friends, neighborhood, community, images on television, magazines, newspapers, books, videos, and music. How do all these factors influence our perception of race?

Write down the different factors that influence your perceptions of these races as listed on the U.S. Census: White, Latino, African American, Native American, Asian American. You do not have to share this list with anyone—it is for you to gain insights into your perceptions of other races and where they come from.

- **Do you know anyone of each race?** How many people?

  - Have you ever participated in any social events with someone of each race?

  - What do you frequently hear about people of each race?

  - What three adjectives would you use to describe people of each race?

  - Where do your strongest impressions of each race come from?

- **Can you find any patterns in your thinking?** Are your impressions about groups that include people you know personally more positive than those groups that don't contain anyone you know? What other patterns can you spot?

Chapter 1 ▶
The Creation of Race

How were white Europeans able to treat Africans with so much cruelty?

White colonists used the concept of race to create a racial hierarchy and justify enslaving Africans to build an international economy and enjoy a comfortable lifestyle.

In America, we look at the world through a lens of race. When you first spot someone coming toward you, what is one of the first things you notice about them? If you're like most people, your mind tends to instinctively try to assign that person to a certain racial group. But the concept of race hasn't always existed.

In the world before race, prejudice against people with certain unchanging characteristics, such as skin color, existed. But social hierarchies were usually based on changeable characteristics, such as class, economic status, nationality, religion, or tribe.

The concept of race began in the fifteenth century with the rise of transatlantic African slavery. European colonists in America used the idea of race to construct an unjust social hierarchy and a race-based system of enslavement.

Let's take a look at how this happened.

EARLY SLAVERY

Since the dawn of civilization, slaves have been at the bottom of the social hierarchy. But before racial categories were created, people of every color and religion, in countries and continents from Britain to China to Africa, had been both enslavers and slaves. In ancient Greece and Rome, slaves were primarily people who had been captured through war, debt, piracy, or kidnapping. During the early Middle Ages, the Vikings regularly enslaved people from Britain, Ireland, and Eastern Europe during raids. Slavery has existed for thousands of years.

The widespread enslavement of Africans began in the seventh century with the Arab slave trade. During the course of several centuries, Arabs trafficked millions of sub-Saharan Africans, along with countless Europeans, primarily Eastern European slaves.

A nineteenth-century engraving showing an Arab slave-trading caravan transporting black African slaves across the Sahara Desert

As the Arab slave trade continued, Africans became more and more strongly equated with slavery.

THE RISE OF AFRICAN SLAVERY

In the fifteenth century, Europeans began exploring the world far and wide. The Portuguese, who were especially talented at shipbuilding and seafaring, took the lead. With visions of glory and riches, they established new trade routes to the East. In 1441, the Portuguese became the first Europeans to explore Africa's west coast. They established partnerships with African rulers, trading European fabrics, brass, and weapons for ivory, gold, and pepper.

The Portuguese set up trading posts throughout the region and colonized several uninhabited islands along the African coast. At first, they focused more on developing sugar and cotton plantations and exploiting African natural resources than developing a slave trade. But when they saw the potential profit in selling humans, their strategy quickly changed.

Africa had a thriving domestic slave trade, as did many other places. Warring kingdoms and tribes sometimes traded their captives to other Africans, as well as to Arabs.

The Portuguese realized that, not only could they make money by selling Africans as slaves, but they could also develop their plantations quickly and cheaply using slave labor. By the 1460s, the Portuguese had fully embraced the slave trade, selling African people to Europeans, along with African ivory and gold.

EUROPEAN PREJUDICE AGAINST AFRICANS

Most Europeans—particularly the English—were almost immediately prejudiced against the physical appearance and way of life of people from Africa. The English began to explore the African coast during the mid-1500s. At this time, they had extremely strict social hierarchies and codes of conduct. The ruling class in England viewed many societies—of any color—that did not meet their standards as inferior.

> The English saw Africans as different from themselves in almost every way.

Writers of the period often described Africans as ape-like, lacking in reason and civility, wildly sexual, and prone to thievery and nakedness. Some writers portrayed African ceremonial customs as "devilish" rituals, which would have disturbed the average English person's Christian sensibilities. These dehumanizing descriptions of Africans were repeated in plays, poems, and stories of the time.[1]

Of all the ways the English found Africans different, they seemed to be most struck by their dark skin color. Like the Portuguese, they began to refer to all sub-Saharan Africans collectively as "Negro" or "black" rather than by their country, kingdom, or tribe of origin. It was also during this period that Europeans slowly began to refer to themselves as "white" in writings.

SLAVE RAIDS

Africans were often taken and sold into slavery after being captured in war, condemned as criminals, or kidnapped through slave raids carried out by African collaborators or Europeans themselves. Some people argue that because Africans sold other Africans to Europeans, Europeans don't need to carry the moral burden of the development of the transatlantic slave trade. What do you think?

The English also had great contempt for the Irish in the sixteenth century, often characterizing them as violent "savages" and expressing contempt for their nomadic lifestyle, scant clothing, and, later, religious differences.

One popular theory of darker skin was that the hot African climate caused Africans to be dark, but once they were in a cooler climate, they would become a "normal" white color. Another was a theory called the "Curse of Ham." In the Bible, Ham was the son of Noah in the story of Noah's Ark. The Bible says Noah cursed Ham to be a "servant of servants" for seeing Noah drunk and naked and for committing an unmentioned offense. In the ninth century, an ancient Jewish text was interpreted as saying that Noah cursed Ham and his descendants to be dark-skinned.

When the English sailed to the New World in the early 1600s, they transported these negative views of Africans with them. They also brought their deep-rooted view of English superiority over people markedly different from themselves.

American slaveholders used the Curse of Ham theory to justify African enslavement. Many Judaism experts say this passage in the Bible was misinterpreted to promote a racist agenda.

RACE REALITY

Research the different meanings of the colors "black" and "white" in the sixteenth and seventeenth centuries. How might framing Africans collectively as "Negro" have influenced European society's perception of them?

THE COLONIZATION OF NORTH AMERICA

In 1607, a group of British men landed in Virginia and established the Jamestown colony. They soon realized that the path to wealth in Virginia lay not in the gold they'd hoped to find, but in agricultural exports. But first, they had to negotiate with the Powhatans, the powerful Algonquian tribe on whose hunting land the British had built their colony.

In the beginning, Native Americans and the English wavered between being allies and enemies. Neither completely trusted the other, but each saw the advantages of having a friendly relationship. The English, though fearful of tales of the "savage" natives, needed the locals to teach them about planting and surviving the wilderness. The Powhatan tribe was wary of the English but hoped English weapons might be useful in defeating rival tribes.

As Europeans encroached more and more upon their land, Native Americans began to realize the threat to their way of life and relations between both groups grew increasingly hostile.

The wars and aggressions between Native Americans and Europeans reinforced the English view of Native Americans as "savages," and led some colonists to believe that enslaving them was the answer. But although thousands of Native Americans did become enslaved in North America, enslavement of the indigenous population never became as widespread as African slavery.

Meanwhile, the colonists at Jamestown learned how to plant tobacco with great success. By 1630, Virginia was exporting a million and a half pounds of tobacco to England. To continue this success, the planters needed cheap labor—and plenty of it.

FIRST AFRICANS IN THE BRITISH COLONIES

American history was forever changed in 1619, when an English warship landed at Port Comfort, Virginia, with 20 or so Africans. The crew sold the Africans to colonists for food and set sail again. These are believed to be the first Africans in the North American colonies. But they weren't necessarily slaves—at least some were indentured servants.

Indentured servants were people who worked for wealthy planters for a certain period of time. They did this in exchange for food and lodging and, in the case of European servants, payment of their voyage to North America.

THE "RED" INDIAN?

The British colonists didn't view Native Americans in the same derogatory light as Africans. They approved of the Native Americans' light skin and hair texture. Colonists' journals sometimes referred to the red dye Native Americans put on their skin, but it had no negative connotation at first. Although the British disliked that the natives weren't Christian and thought them too violent, they were optimistic that "Indians" could eventually be converted to English ways. Later, as relations between Europeans and Native Americans worsened, the colonists placed more emphasis on their differences and the Native Americans were eventually derogatorily called "red" men.

Massachusetts became the first colony to legalize slavery in 1641.

Once the servants completed their contracts, they received freedom dues—a payment of land, supplies, clothes, and a weapon—and were released to live their lives. In these early years, records show that some Africans received freedom dues after completing their contract terms and became free.

Despite the similar status of Africans and European servants, planters treated Africans more harshly. The story of John Punch (dates unknown) demonstrates this. An African indentured servant, he ran away from his Virginia contract holder in 1640 with three European servants. After being captured, the white servants were punished by having their contracts extended by four years. John Punch was a servant for the rest of his life—in effect, made a slave.

CREATION OF A SOCIAL HIERARCHY

By the mid-seventeenth century, colonists became increasingly determined to establish a social hierarchy that firmly placed Africans at the bottom. From the 1660s onward, the colonies passed dozens of laws with explicit racial discriminations. Known as slave codes, these laws laid the groundwork for ensuring white domination and a system of race-based chattel slavery.

Slave codes varied slightly among the colonies, but all of them whittled away the rights of Africans until they had almost none. The codes forbade enslaved Africans from possessing weapons or property, making contracts, testifying against Europeans, or assembling in large groups. Most importantly, the codes established that enslaved Africans, and sometimes Native Americans, were the legal property of their enslaver and were enslaved for life.

For the first time, the laws also established slavery as hereditary. In 1662, Virginia law stated that any child born to an enslaved African woman would also be enslaved.

Having a child's status pass through their mother offered two enormous advantages to slaveholders. They could enlarge their enslaved population through procreation. Plus, it officially linked African ancestry to enslavement, making it difficult for people to think of one without the other.

PROHIBITION OF INTERRACIAL ALLIANCES

Slave codes not only stripped Africans of their rights, they also criminalized interracial alliances and intimate relationships. For example, in 1661, Virginia law stated that any English servant caught running away in the company of "negroes" would be punished by serving for the time of the "absence of the negro."

Maryland law stated that any white woman who married an enslaved African would also become enslaved, as would her children. In some colonies, priests who married interracial couples, including Native Americans, would be severely fined.

Laws designed to drive a wedge between whites and blacks increased after an event known as Bacon's Rebellion. In 1676, a Virginia planter named Nathaniel Bacon (1647–1676) led an army of white servants, farmers, black servants, and enslaved Africans in a violent campaign against Native Americans.

The new hereditary law was a huge break with traditional British common law, which for centuries had said that children took their father's status. But the colonists saw it as necessary. This old tradition didn't suit their new needs.

THE BUTLERS

Interracial marriages brought severe consequences in the colonies, but some couples accepted the punishment. Famously, Eleanor Butler (c.1665–unknown), a white servant known as "Irish Nell," married an enslaved African named Charles Butler (dates unknown) in 1681. Her act shocked colonists because it meant she would become enslaved, as would her children. Still, Eleanor insisted she'd "rather have Charles" than her freedom. A few of the couple's children later managed to win their freedom.

When Virginia's governor denounced Nathaniel Bacon's action, the planter attacked the colony itself.

His interracial forces burned Jamestown to the ground and continued fighting for months. The rebellion faded when its leader died of dysentery three months later, but wealthy planters were apparently shaken by the vision of a racially united underclass. Poorer whites began to be granted more rights, while Africans increasingly lost theirs.

SYSTEMATIC DEHUMANIZATION

When someone is dehumanized, other people don't consider their feelings or well-being, as though they are no longer human. This is what Europeans did to Africans, in addition to passing laws that kept them from being free.

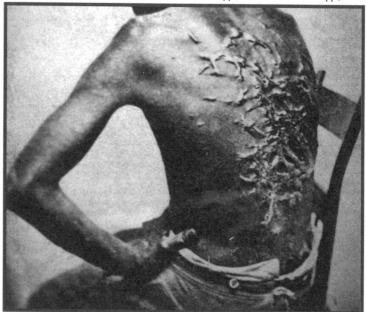

The scars of a whipped slave from Mississippi, 1863

SELF-PURCHASE

A small percentage of Africans managed to obtain freedom through "self-purchase." They persuaded their enslavers to pay them for performing specialized work, such as carpentry or sewing, then saved enough money to purchase themselves and sometimes their families. Although saving took them many years, and there was no guarantee their owners would be honest and honor the agreement, many considered it worth the risk.

Enslavers also maintained their dominance with violence. Beatings, whippings, burnings, and mutilations could occur anywhere, anytime.

From the moment Africans were enslaved, they were treated as though they weren't human and didn't feel pain, fear, sadness, longing, or love.

Back on the African shores, slave traders crammed terrified Africans into ships in filthy conditions, where they sometimes had to remain for as long as two months. Upon reaching the colonies, Africans were forced to stand, shackled, on an auction block, while European enslavers prodded and evaluated their bodies to assess their work potential. African women were valued for their ability to "breed," and slaveholders regularly tore apart African families by selling fathers, mothers, children, or siblings to different enslavers whenever it suited them.

MAINTAINING WHITE SUPREMACY

By the mid-1700s, race-based slavery had become firmly established. But slaveholders were anxious. Slavery was vital to the economy, particularly in the South. Because their way of life depended heavily on forced labor, enslavers lived in constant fear of uprisings.

Slaveholders knew if they weren't vigilant, a rebellion could occur right beneath their noses. They needed more than laws to keep the system of racial domination they had created. So, they came up with measures to keep the enslaved population down.

In the early 1700s, Southern enslavers instituted slave patrols. These were groups of white men who policed enslaved Africans by randomly searching their homes for weapons, breaking up gatherings, looking for runaways, and listening for whispers of rebellion. They were authorized to physically punish Africans and any "suspicious" whites.

Read the personal narratives of five enslaved people who self-purchased. How much did they pay for their liberty? What do their stories suggest about the race relations of the period? What contradictions are present?

national humanities center buying freedom

One of the more deceptive ways slaveholders attempted to maintain supremacy over Africans was by spreading negative stories about the African character.

Although Africans were forced to work under cruel conditions so their slaveholders would make money, enslavers characterized Africans as lazy. Even as enslavers denied Africans education, they insisted that Africans were unintelligent. Although slaveholders frequently raped African women, they portrayed African men as sexual threats. And even as enslavers stole the liberty and life of millions of Africans, they made Africans out as thieves.

By repeating these harmful narratives about Africans, the colonists created the idea that Europeans were morally superior and that oppressing Africans was justified.

The first slave revolt occurred in Manhattan, New York, in 1712.

Slaves in South Carolina, 1862

AFRICAN RESISTANCE

Enslavers' efforts to crush Africans into total submission didn't work as well as they hoped. Africans found ways to rebel in one way or another. They often engaged in "everyday resistance," or tiny acts of defiance that subtly undermined an enslaver's power. Sometimes, they worked slowly or broke tools. Occasionally, they faked an inability to understand simple instructions, forcing their irritated enslavers to repeat themselves again and again.

Africans also resisted by finding ways to achieve things that society or the law denied them. Sometimes, they secretly taught themselves how to read, occasionally with the help of white allies. They called each other by their chosen names, not ones their slaveholders had given them. Although not legally allowed to get married, they created their own marriage ceremonies.

Finding pleasure in life was also a form of resistance. Enslaved Africans formed their own communities and traditions. Although they came from diverse areas of Africa and often spoke different languages, they had cultural commonalities, such as a love of music, dancing, and storytelling, that drew them together.

Sometimes, their form of resistance was violent. Over the decades, enslaved Africans organized multiple revolts. These rebellions sometimes brought death to enslavers and hope to the enslaved, even though, ultimately, the colonists were always able to quash the uprisings.

Slavery seemed set in stone, but ideas were slowly changing. What would it take for slavery in the United States to become a thing of the past? We'll take a look in the next chapter.

Phillis Wheatley (1753–1784), whose enslavers taught her to read and write as a child, published a book of poems at age 18 and could read Latin and Greek. Read some of Phillis's poems at this website.

🔍 Phillis Wheatley poem hunter

KEY QUESTIONS

- **What might American race relations be like now if the colonists had not created slave codes?**

- **Can you think of any examples of people dehumanizing other groups of people today?**

- **Why did slaveholders outlaw or prohibit the education of slaves?**

BY THE LAW

Laws communicate the behaviors and attitudes that society considers acceptable. Review the following excerpt from Virginia's slave code and consider the various attitudes and actions that were acceptable in colonial America and their impact on race relations.

 csulb Virginia slave laws

VOCAB LAB

Write down what you think each word means. What root words can you find to help you? What does the context of the word tell you?

civility, **contempt**, **dehumanize**, **hierarchy**, **indigenous**, **interracial**, **slave**, **slave code**, and **stereotype**.

Compare your definitions with those of your friends or classmates. Did you all come up with the same meanings? Turn to the text and glossary if you need help.

* **In analyzing the code, write out answers to the following questions.**

  * What behaviors did the slave code consider important enough to regulate?

  * Do any of these laws use dehumanizing language? How so?

  * In what ways did these laws dictate the behavior of the colonists and not Africans?

  * How did the laws reflect the importance of slavery to the economy?

  * How did these laws foster the idea that whites were superior?

* **If you were starting a brand-new community or club, what kind of behaviors and attitudes would you find acceptable?** Write a code of laws for your community.

> **To investigate more,** consider the ways in which race was a social construct. Research the situations of Anthony Johnson and Elizabeth Key (1630–1665). Elizabeth was one of the first people to sue the colonies for her freedom and win. In what ways do their circumstances reflect the arbitrary construction of race? What contradictions are inherent in their situations?

Chapter 2 ▶
An Interracial Fight for Freedom

HAVE RACE RELATIONS CHANGED FROM EARLY AMERICA UNTIL NOW?

How and why did the American institution of slavery end?

As the antislavery movement gained momentum, Northern and Southern states became dangerously divided over the issue, triggering the Civil War.

In the late eighteenth century, race relations saw a shift as a growing number of people began the long fight to abolish slavery. The success of the antislavery movement was due to the combined efforts of free and enslaved African Americans who fought for freedom and the British-American allies who used their positions, privilege, and voices to support them.

While resistance to slavery stirred for hundreds of years, the abolitionist movement can be traced back to a sale that one man found deeply unsettling. In 1742, a store clerk named John Woolman (1720–1722) was asked to write a sale receipt for an enslaved African woman. He did so, but the inhumanity of the transaction inspired him to dedicate the rest of his life to the cause of abolishing slavery.

He began traveling around the colonies, trying to convince slaveholders of the incompatibility of slavery and Christian principles. This marked one of the first lasting efforts of a colonist to end slavery.

John Woolman was a Quaker, a member of a Christian religious group that had settled in the colonies during the seventeenth century. By 1761, Quakers had prohibited slavery among their members. They remained one of the most loyal allies to Africans throughout the long fight for freedom.

Quakers weren't the only ones reflecting on human liberty. Colonists were also turning their attention to what it meant to be free. They were growing increasingly angered by King George III's (1738–1820) authority over the colonies. In 1763, the English king began to impose costly restrictions and demands upon the colonists, including an expensive tax on popular goods such as sugar and tea.

The colonists were furious that a king across an ocean should have such power over their lives without any representatives to speak for their interests. Calling themselves patriots, they began to argue passionately for freedom from British rule and the ability to determine their own form of government. The king's broad authority, many colonists insisted, was like slavery.

AFRICANS FIGHT FOR FREEDOM

Africans, enslaved and free, listened to news of a revolution with hope—maybe revolution could bring freedom to their people, one way or another. Seizing the momentum, they tried to achieve their own independence in multiple ways.

Some Africans thought that aligning themselves with the British would bring freedom. In November 1775, the royal governor of Virginia, Lord Dunmore (1730–1809), offered freedom to enslaved Africans if they fought with loyalist British troops. Thousands of African men attempted to answer the governor's call, and several hundred were successful.

RACE REALITY

Some patriots recognized the hypocrisy of calling for freedom while keeping one-sixth of the population enslaved. Abigail Adams (1744–1818), wife of future president John Adams (1764–1818), wrote in 1775, "It always appeared a most iniquitous scheme to me—to fight ourselves for what we are daily robbing and plundering from those who have as good a right to freedom as we have."[1]

Soldiers in Uniform (c. 1781 and 1784)

credit: Jean Baptiste Antoine de Verger

RACE REALITY

The American Revolution was the last time the military permitted racially integrated forces for 170 years. The next time black and white Americans would fight side-by-side would be in the Korean War in 1950. Why do you think there was such a gap in history?

Several thousand more put their hope of freedom in fighting with the patriots. At the beginning of the war, General George Washington (1732–1799) banned all black men from fighting because he was fearful that arming Africans could lead to rebellions. By 1777, however, he began admitting free blacks into the army. Northern colonies began promising enslaved people freedom if they fought for the revolutionaries.

Military authorities tended to turn a blind eye to runaway enslaved Africans enlisting as revolutionary soldiers.

By the revolution's end, approximately 15,000 Africans had served in the revolutionary forces. Many won their freedom because of it.

THE WOLF BY THE EAR

As the revolution raged in 1776, Thomas Jefferson (1743–1826) was busy drafting the Declaration of Independence. Despite enslaving hundreds of people on his own plantation, he recognized the immorality of human bondage and thunderously condemned it.

Nonetheless, the future U.S. president didn't support emancipation, or the freeing of all slaves—he felt that too much bad history existed between blacks and whites to live peaceably together in freedom. He once remarked in a letter, "[W]e have the wolf by the ear, and we can neither hold him, nor safely let him go. Justice is in one scale, and self-preservation in the other."[2]

By the time of the Constitutional Convention in 1787, when the Founding Fathers met to draft the guiding principles of the new country, the question of slavery was such a sensitive topic that the United States was in danger of falling apart before it was born. To many Northern delegates, slavery was a dying, immoral institution that America didn't need. For Southerners, slavery was both tradition and their bread-and-butter.

> Ultimately, the delegates decided not to even mention slavery, except for a few vague references, in the Constitution.

Starting with Vermont in 1777, the newly ratified Northern states began abolishing slavery. Some abolished it through their constitutions, while others did it gradually, first freeing children born after a certain date, then allowing for the freedom of children upon the age of maturity. Why do you think some states did this so gradually?

Read the text of the first draft of the Declaration of Independence, in which Thomas Jefferson condemned the institution of slavery. What might race relations have been like if Jefferson's reference had remained in the final version?

 LOC rough draft

THREE-FIFTHS COMPROMISE

The delegates couldn't agree on whether to count slaves among the population when deciding on congressional representatives. Northerners argued that, as property, they shouldn't count at all. Southerners wanted slaves to count as a full vote because then they'd have more representatives. As a compromise, the delegates agreed that each enslaved person would count as three-fifths of a person toward representation.

THE COLONIZATION PROJECT

In 1816, a group of antislavery whites seized upon the idea of sending black people to West Africa. They created the American Colonization Society (ACS), which established a colony in West Africa called Liberia for this purpose. The idea appealed to some free blacks who were sick of the constant racism and discrimination, but most furiously objected to the idea. By the 1820s, many free black people were a few generations removed from Africa and considered themselves American. Moreover, some felt they had a moral right to live in America since the toil of African slaves had helped the country to grow rich. In the end, more than 13,000 free black Americans eventually emigrated to Liberia during the nineteenth century.

Still, the North was certainly not free of racism. Many schools, churches, and restaurants were segregated. Interracial marriage was outlawed. Black people were usually hired for only the most lowly jobs. White property owners didn't want to rent or sell to black people, so blacks were often forced to live in overcrowded, run-down ghettos—then condemned by white society for living in slums. Black men were either barred from voting outright or blocked from voting through restrictions such as needing to own property.

As the number of free blacks swelled in the nineteenth century, Northern political leaders grew concerned. Free blacks threatened the social hierarchy by demanding equal treatment. Many worried it was only a matter of time before free blacks incited a major slave rebellion.

THE ANTISLAVERY MOVEMENT

Until the mid-nineteenth century, the antislavery movement had been mainly a segregated effort, with blacks and whites each forming their own abolitionist societies. William Lloyd Garrison (1805–1879) began to change this.

William was a writer, editor, and fervent antislavery proponent. Unlike many of his compatriots, he not only advocated for immediate emancipation and rejected colonization, but he also had the so-called radical idea that African Americans were entitled to legal and social equality. This was markedly different from the opinions of his fellow abolitionists.

In 1831, William formed the interracial New England Anti-Slavery Society. He also founded *The Liberator*, an influential newspaper that published aggressive antislavery articles every week from 1831 until slavery was abolished in 1865.

Women also played a critical role in the antislavery movement. Of these, one of the most famous was Sojourner Truth (c. 1797–1883), who became an antislavery and women's rights advocate after her son was kidnapped from the North and enslaved in the South, just days before he was to be emancipated. Although enslaved herself, Sojourner successfully used the courts to bring her son home.

Hundreds of other abolitionists, black and white, took great risks to champion the cause of freedom, particularly the countless people who helped form the Underground Railroad.

THE UNDERGROUND RAILROAD

The Underground Railroad was an informal network of people who helped enslaved African Americans reach freedom in Northern states or Canada. These people served different roles—some provided shelter and food, some acted as "conductors," or guides, others served as coordinators. The railroad was truly an interracial cooperation, composed mainly of African Americans, many of them former or fugitive slaves, and sympathetic white abolitionists, often Quakers.

Participating in the railroad was dangerous, especially for former slaves, but many fugitives helped others escape, time and time again. The most famous of these is Harriet Tubman (c. 1822–1913), a hugely courageous woman who escaped from slavery in 1849, but returned to the South at least a dozen times to help lead others to freedom. Neither she nor those she helped were ever caught.

Antislavery advocate Frederick Douglass (c. 1818–1895) credited *The Liberator* for his desire to become an abolitionist. Having escaped from slavery in 1838, he went on to become one of the most powerful antislavery activists in history.

RACE REALITY

Congress abolished the international slave trade in 1808, increasing the value of the domestic slave trade.

Henry Box Brown shipped himself north to escape from slavery.

RESURRECTION OF HENRY BOX BROWN.

credit: William Still

By the time the Civil War ended in 1865, the Underground Railroad had helped between 25,000 and 40,000 flee bondage.

JUSTIFYING SLAVERY

In the South, slavery was as strong as ever. After Eli Whitney's (1765–1825) cotton gin came onto the market in 1794, the demand for slave labor increased. Cotton quickly became America's most valuable export.

But it was becoming harder for slaveholders to ignore the increasingly loud demands for emancipation from abolitionists. Their reaction was to double down on justifications for slavery. They claimed various passages in the Bible supported it, and that God intended for African Americans to be enslaved.

They also argued that if African Americans were emancipated, they would violently turn on white people. Enslavers pointed warningly to slave rebellions as a chilling vision of what society might become if the enslaved were freed.

More popular still was the paternalism argument—that slavery was good for African Americans. They claimed that without the structure of slavery, black people would be utterly helpless.

MANIFEST DESTINY

As the issue of slavery continued to boil, white Americans continued to seek new land to settle. Throughout the eighteenth century, European colonizers increasingly encroached upon the lands of indigenous people. To keep the peace, many tribes reluctantly entered into land settlement treaties with the colonizers. But in the nineteenth century, the concept of Manifest Destiny gripped white America.

> Manifest Destiny was the belief that white Americans were meant to expand across the entire North American continent.

In 1830, President Andrew Jackson (1767–1845) signed into law the Indian Removal Act. This law gave the president the authority to grant to Native Americans wildlands west of the Mississippi River in exchange for the land Native Americans had already cultivated in the southeast.

Some tribes left peacefully, but several tribes refused. The government forcibly removed these tribes in a series of brutal marches in the 1830s, displacing them west in what is now Oklahoma. A few decades later, the government took back most of the Oklahoma lands as well.

TRAIL OF TEARS

The Native American Cherokee Nation had agreed to live in northeast Georgia based on a 1791 treaty with the U.S. government. When Georgia discovered gold on Cherokee land in 1828, it seized the land, divided it up, and sold it in a lottery to whites. The Cherokee fought this action in court, but in 1838, the government forced some 15,000 Cherokees from their land, marching them from Georgia to Oklahoma. The government, however, failed to provide adequate supplies to the tribe during the long trek, and about 4,000 Cherokee died of starvation, cold, and disease. The Cherokee called this march "The Place Where They Cried." Today, it's commonly known as the Trail of Tears. You can read some stories of families who were on the trail at this website.

🔍 UALR exhibit
family stories

THE FUGITIVE SLAVE ACT OF 1850

The Missouri Compromise of 1820 prohibited slavery north of the 36-degree, 30-minute latitude line to keep a balance between slave and free states. But as new states and territories were added to the Union, the balance was in danger. Southern states threatened to secede and leave the Union if slave states were not admitted.

To appease the South, the U.S. Congress agreed to a series of compromises, including the Fugitive Slave Act, which forced all white citizens, even Northerners, to return runaways to their enslavers or face prison or a steep fine. Slave-catchers swarmed the North, looking for fugitives. Sometimes, they kidnapped free blacks to bring them South.

Thousands of free blacks fled to Canada to avoid the slave-catchers, while others formed groups to help protect fugitive slaves.

Northern whites were furious, and more of them put themselves in danger to help African Americans become and stay free.

By the late 1850s, the North and South were fiercely divided over whether the federal government had the power to curtail slavery. The dispute was split along political lines. Democrats were generally proslavery and against the federal government deciding on behalf of the states. But a brand-new antislavery party called Republicans believed the government had the right to decide. One of its earliest members was a lawyer named Abraham Lincoln (1809–1865).

UNCLE TOM'S CABIN

In 1854, a white woman called Harriet Beecher Stowe (1811–1896) published the antislavery book, *Uncle Tom's Cabin*. The book showed the inherent cruelty of slavery through characters with whom readers could emotionally connect. Its subtle message was extremely effective and pushed countless whites firmly into the antislavery camp.

John Brown's raid on Harper's Ferry

credit: Frank Leslie's illustrated newspaper, 1859

Tensions heightened when an enslaved man named Dred Scott (c. 1799–1858) sued for his freedom after his enslaver died while living in a free state. In 1857, the U.S. Supreme Court ruled that the slave had no right to sue because black people, whether enslaved or free, "had no rights a white man was bound to respect." To the shock of many, the court also ruled that the federal government couldn't deprive people of their property—including enslaved people—and thus, slavery couldn't be restricted in Western territories.

When Abraham Lincoln was elected president in 1860, Southerners didn't trust his promise not to abolish slavery. In early 1861, nine states in the South seceded from the Union and formed a new nation, the Confederate States of America. The first shots of the Civil War were fired on April 12, 1961.

Abraham Lincoln warned that the Supreme Court might next rule that states couldn't deprive people of their property at all, which would open the door to nationwide slavery. Northern Democrats increasingly joined the Republican Party.

THE CIVIL WAR

When the Civil War began, African Americans once again saw the opportunity to fight for their freedom. Free black men lined up to join the Union army, but were turned away.

President Lincoln was initially afraid that more Southern states would secede if he accepted black soldiers, but he changed his mind in 1862. Approximately 200,000 African Americans would eventually serve in segregated regiments.[4]

On January 1, 1863, President Lincoln issued the Emancipation Proclamation, declaring all slaves in the Confederate States free. Abolitionists and enslaved African Americans celebrated, although the announcement didn't really free anyone, since the Confederate States didn't consider themselves under the federal government's control. It was clear that the abolition of slavery hinged on a Union victory, which finally came when Confederate troops surrendered on April 9, 1865.

But, as Frederick Douglass wrote, "Work does not end with the abolition of slavery, but only begins." Next, we'll look at the Reconstruction era, when the battle for freedom turned into a battle for equality.

RACE REALITY

During the Civil War, Harriet Tubman served as a spy for the Union army, going behind enemy lines to recruit slaves to report on Confederate troop movements.

KEY QUESTIONS

- **What role did economics play in the idea that slavery was justified?**

- **Do you think it was difficult for white abolitionists to stand up for their beliefs? Have you ever taken a stand that was unpopular? What gave you the courage to do so?**

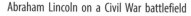

Abraham Lincoln on a Civil War battlefield

SLAVE NARRATIVES

During the eighteenth and nineteenth centuries, dozens of former slaves wrote autobiographies about their own experiences. Known as "slave narratives," those written before emancipation served an important role in turning whites toward abolitionism.

- **You can find many slave narratives at this website.**   documenting American south slave narratives

- **Choose a slave narrative to read from one of these people and answer the following questions.**

  - What steps does the author take to authenticate his or her writings? Why?

  - Does this narrative challenge your assumptions about slaves or slavery? How?

  - Identify three passages in the narrative that might have turned whites against slavery. What makes these passages persuasive?

  - What passages would slavery supporters use to justify slavery?

  - Do you think your author would be for or against colonization? Why?

  - What do you think freedom meant to your author? What did the idea of equality mean to them?

To investigate more, research the arguments for and against colonization in Liberia from the African American perspective. You may want to begin your research by focusing on Samuel Cornish (1795–1858) and John Brown Russwurm (1799–1851), who were founders of *Freedom's Journal*, the first African American newspaper. The two had differing attitudes toward colonization. Team up with a classmate, each choosing a side to argue, and debate the matter.

VOCAB LAB 📖

Write down what you think each word means. What root words can you find to help you? What does the context of the word tell you?

abolitionist, **displace**, **emancipation**, **emigrate**, **fugitive**, **hypocrisy**, and **secede**.

Compare your definitions with those of your friends or classmates. Did you all come up with the same meanings? Turn to the text and glossary if you need help.

MASS DEPOPULATION OF NATIVE AMERICANS

Before Europeans arrived in 1492, an estimated 54 million Native Americans were living in what is now the United States. Within decades, millions died due to European diseases, war, and displacement. By 1890, the Native American population had dropped to 228,000. Although historians debate whether the devastation of the Native American population was an intentional genocide, they do not dispute that Europeans caused the dramatic depopulation, whether by acting purposefully, accidentally, or with reckless indifference.

* **Trace the history of one of the Native American tribes.** Choose between the Cherokee, Iroquois, Mohawk, Seminole, Sioux, Comanche, Algonquin, or Cheyenne.

* **Make a timeline of significant events in the tribe's history.** These should include important relationships with colonists or Americans, treaties made with the U.S. government, wars, peacetimes, displacements, and current status.

* **Research the culture of your chosen tribe.** How did the historical events affect that culture?

> **To investigate more,** write a short play or scene about an event in your chosen tribe's history that affected its lifestyle or population. Incorporate differing views tribe members may have had and how they may have felt looking to the future.

Chapter 3 ▶
A Step Toward Equality

"WE HAVE THE WOLF BY THE EAR." —THOMAS JEFFERSON

How did things change for African Americans after the Civil War?

Reconstruction was a period from 1865 to 1877 that focused on reunifying the country and rebuilding the South. But for race relations, this period was a battle between those fighting to make African Americans full and equal citizens and those determined to keep them subordinated.

After the Civil War, the shock of slavery's end shook race relations, particularly in the South. White Southerners had known African Americans only as tools to be owned and controlled, while African Americans were thrilled and determined to make the most of their freedom.

The South was in ruin, the landscape littered with destroyed buildings. But, even amid such wreckage, there were glimmers of joy. Former slaves were ecstatic to be free. As the Union armies overtook Southern cities in early 1865, freed African Americans followed behind them, cheering and singing. In Richmond, Virginia, when Union forces arrived, 4,000 black people took part in a massive parade, some carrying a banner reading, "We Know No Master But Ourselves."

But African Americans knew that true freedom meant having equal opportunities and rights. As Henry Adams, a former slave, expressed in 1865, "If I cannot do like a white man, I am not free."[1]

FREE AT LAST

Many of the newly free left the plantations they'd been confined to in search of cities and towns where they might find paid work—or just to experience the freedom to do so. They found it astonishing to go wherever they pleased without having to obtain permission or risk arrest by a slave patroller.

Thousands searched for lost loved ones—parents, children, and siblings who had been sold by their enslavers years earlier. Many searched by placing ads in black newspapers, while others searched on foot. Black couples, finally able to marry legally, did so, knowing for the first time that they could not be sold away from one another.

Education was one of the most important priorities for the newly free. Knowing that education was key to a better life, African Americans, from the young to the very old, sought out schools in droves. Black people with even a little education rushed to set up makeshift classes anywhere they could—abandoned warehouses, churches, and even former slave markets. They formed societies to raise money to purchase land for more schools, while black carpenters donated their labor to construct school houses. By 1867, almost every county in the South had a school for black students.

"40 ACRES AND A MULE"

Perhaps second to education, freedpeople also desired land. With land, they could grow food to eat or crops to sell, which meant economic security and independence from white control.

African Americans who had attended black universities in the North headed South to teach, along with many Northern white missionaries and aid societies. Supplies were often scarce—sometimes no more than a Bible and a dictionary—but all were happy to learn whatever they could.

RACE REALITY

Southern whites were stunned by the loss of the war. Their entire way of life had been upended. Once-prosperous plantations were now smoking ruins. Without slave labor to put them right, planters couldn't imagine a way forward.

As one freedman from Charleston, South Carolina, told a reporter, "Gib us our own land and we take care of ourselves, but widout land de ole masses can hire us or starve us as dey please."[2]

At first, freedpeople had hopes that they would receive property from the government. In January 1865, Union General William Tecumseh Sherman (1820–1891) issued Special Field Order No. 15, which set aside about 400,000 acres of coastal property from South Carolina to Florida for freedmen. The land had been confiscated from wealthy planters during the war.

The order gave land to freedmen in 40-acre parcels, along with supplies. It also suggested that the army would lend people mules to help cultivate the land. By June 15, 1865, the Freedmen's Bureau had settled 40,000 black families on this and other confiscated or abandoned Southern land.

But the situation was not to last. In the fall of 1865, the new U.S. president, Andrew Johnson (1808–1875), decided to return the confiscated property and grant amnesty to any Southerner who promised loyalty to the Union and support for emancipation. Thousands of wealthy planters asked for Johnson's pardon. The government promptly gave them the land back, evicting the tens of thousands of newly settled African Americans. General Sherman later said he'd only intended to grant the land temporarily. Sadly, this was just the first sign of changes for the worse.

By late 1865, the euphoria that freedom had brought had worn off. Cities were overcrowded and jobs scarce. Many freedpeople were facing starvation. Reluctantly, they began to drift back to the plantations they detested, thinking that at least they'd get paid for their work.

Read a copy of Field Order No. 15 here. If you were a freedperson, what would you believe the order granted? Why?

 order by commander freedmen

THE KU KLUX KLAN

A group of former Confederate soldiers formed a secret social club. Supposedly, the KKK was formed only to play pranks on freedpeople, but the club quickly morphed into a white supremacist organization whose purpose was to keep black people subjugated through extreme violence and intimidation.

Meanwhile, whites were enraged by how quickly black people flung off the restrictions that society had forced upon them. One Southern woman indignantly described how some African Americans "took to calling their former owners by their last name without any title before it" and failed to remove their hats before speaking to her. Others complained of blacks no longer giving way when walking on a road or refusing to do fieldwork.[4]

The perceived humiliation of having to treat black Americans as equals guided Southerners' method of reconstructing the South. Slavery was legally over, but they would try to recreate it as best they could.

CONVICT LEASING

For Southerners, the key to rebuilding the South was restoring the plantations. Once again, they needed plenty of workers. Some towns and countries began to make deals with local planters to lease out their black male convicts to work on plantations.

Black men, who, as property, were rarely imprisoned during slavery, began to fill the jails, usually for petty offenses such as vagrancy, theft and gambling. Even children as young as six years old were imprisoned. Whites, on the other hand, tended not to be imprisoned at all, except for the most serious of crimes.

The conditions for the prisoners were horrible and inhumane. They were beaten and forced to work for hours in blazing heat. They lived in filthy, germ-ridden conditions. Thousands died from disease, exhaustion, heat stroke, and other ailments.

THE FREEDMEN'S BUREAU

In 1865, Congress created the Bureau of Refugees, Freedmen and Abandoned Lands. The so-called Freedmen's Bureau was a temporary measure designed to help freedpeople settle into their new lives. The Freedmen's Bureau issued food and clothes, established schools and hospitals, helped reunite black families, provided jobs, and reviewed labor contracts, among many other things. Although it was discontinued in 1869, the Freedmen's Bureau set in place lasting legacies, including historically black schools such as Howard University and Morehouse College, which are still highly respected institutions today.

Male prisoners working in a field in Mississippi, 1911

SLAVE MYTH

Even today, some people say slavery wasn't so bad because some slaves were "treated well" and provided with food and shelter. A post-war Northern reporter implied this when he asked a freedman who had never been beaten why he considered himself mistreated as a slave. The freeman replied, "I was mistreated because I was kept in slavery." What did he mean? What mistreatment is built into the institution of slavery?

Some were murdered outright. No one cared. As one "employer" put it in 1883, "[T]hese convicts, we don't own 'em. One dies, get another."[5]

Convict leasing was just part of the plan. White Southerners also passed a series of laws, known as "Black Codes," which tried to force blacks back into plantation work.

For example, the South Carolina code prohibited freedpeople from working as anything except a farmer or servant, unless they paid a tax that ranged from $10 to $100—a fortune at the time. Mississippi required all black people to have a year-long written employment contract with a white employer or be imprisoned for vagrancy.

With these Black Codes, African Americans understood that white society was trying to bring back slavery without calling it that. Many felt disheartened by how little power they had to fight it. But others sought powerful allies.

In Washington, DC, some politicians were more than willing to take up the cause of the newly free. These were the Radical Republicans, a group of congressmen committed to giving equal rights and opportunities to all Americans, regardless of color.

Although President Johnson was in charge of Reconstruction, it was the Radicals who pushed for the creation of the Freedmen's Bureau to help the newly free after slavery. It was also thanks to the Radicals that the states ratified the Thirteenth Amendment, the formal abolition of slavery, in December 1865. They believed the federal government had to help protect black people's rights or blacks would never truly be free.

The Radicals created the nation's first civil rights bill. This bill declared all U.S.-born persons to be citizens, without regard to race, color, or previous condition of slavery or servitude. Many politicians didn't support the bill, however, including President Johnson. In 1866, he wrote, with respect to the bill, "This is a country for white men, and by God, as long as I am President, it shall be a government for white men."[6]

> But Congress passed the bill over Johnson's veto. The Civil Rights Act became law in April 1866.

GROWING RACIAL VIOLENCE

Southerners were furious over both the implications of the Civil Rights Act and the fact that the federal government was exercising control over their states. These political and racial tensions exploded into extreme violence against African Americans all around the South, even to the point of mass murder.

The most prominent Radical leaders were Senator Charles Sumner (1811–1874) of Massachusetts and Representative Thaddaeus Stevens (1792–1868) of Pennsylvania.

CARPETBAGGERS AND SCALAWAGS

The Ku Klux Klan violently targeted whites who supported black advancement, especially teachers. "Carpetbagger" was the derisive nickname for Northerners who came south to help freedpeople. "Scalawags" were white Southerners who voted Republican or supported Reconstruction policies. Carpetbaggers and scalawags suffered constant harassment and beatings and were sometimes killed.

For example, in May 1866, an altercation between a white policeman and a black former soldier in Memphis, Tennessee, turned into a three-day riot. White mobs raged through the city burning or vandalizing more than 100 African American homes, churches, and schools. Forty-six black people and two whites were killed, five black women were raped, and more than 200 people were injured.

No one was arrested.

Northerners were horrified by the violence in the South. Convinced that Johnson's handling of Reconstruction wasn't working, the public voted in a two-thirds majority Republican Congress in 1866. The Radicals took over Reconstruction.

A STEP TOWARD EQUALITY

The Republicans quickly passed a series of acts known as the Reconstruction Act of 1867. The acts set the terms under which the rebelling Southern states could be fully readmitted to the Union. It required the states to redraft their constitutions, dissolve their all-white governments, hold new elections, and ratify the Fourteenth Amendment.

The Reconstruction Act also divided the Southern states into five military districts, and more than 200,000 soldiers were sent to the South to protect the freedmen's right to vote. Under the watchful eye of federal troops, black men in the South voted for the first time in the fall of 1867.

The issue to be decided was whether to hold conventions to draft a new constitution and elect delegates. All the states voted to hold a convention. Many black delegates, along with white, were elected in every Southern state. The new constitutions drafted were the result of an interracial effort.

MASS SHOOTING

A few months after the riot in Tennessee, policemen, firemen, and other white citizens opened fire on almost 200 black men who were marching in support of a Republican state constitutional convention at the Mechanic's Institute in New Orleans, Louisiana. Nearly 50 black people and three white Republicans were killed and dozens of others were injured.

The new constitutions were very progressive. They all established the right of every adult male citizen to vote, founded public education school systems for all children, created a range of social welfare programs for the poor and disabled, and outlawed the Black Codes.

Tens of thousands of freedmen across the South turned up to vote despite opposition from white people. With the black vote, the pro-equality Republican Party took control of state governments.

BLACK POLITICAL POWER

During the next several years, more than 1,500 African Americans were elected to public office in Southern states. Between 1868 and 1877, 16 black men served as U.S. congressmen and two served in the U.S. Senate. For the first time, African Americans were able to contribute to political conversations and were able to voice the perspectives and concerns of their community.

THE FOURTEENTH AMENDMENT

On July 9, 1868, the states ratified the Fourteenth Amendment, which guaranteed the right and privileges of citizenship to all persons born or naturalized in the United States, except for untaxed Native Americans. Native Americans would not win the right to be considered American citizens until 1924. Why did they have to wait so long?

Black politicians in 1872

credit: Currier and Ives, 1872

THE FIRST COLORED SENATOR AND REPRESENTATIVES.
In the 41ˢᵗ and 42ⁿᵈ Congress of the United States.

Read a spontaneous speech by U.S. Congressman Joseph Rainey (1832–1887), a former barber, about racism. What do you think his white congressional colleagues thought?

neglected voices NYU

Although white Southerners at the time portrayed African American public servants as an ignorant, incompetent, and corrupt bunch of men, history has shown otherwise. The vast majority of black public servants took their roles very seriously and performed competently.

Many white Southerners, however, refused to see anything black politicians did in a positive way. They didn't want to share any social, economic, or political power with black people.

DOMESTIC TERRORISM

After freedmen began to vote, the already frequent incidents of violence against African Americans increased greatly as whites tried to reinstate their power. The Ku Klux Klan (KKK) and other white supremacist organizations now had thousands of members across the South.

The KKK moved in groups, with men disguising their faces with hooded masks and carrying guns. They usually attacked at night, rousing people from their beds, beating some and outright murdering others. Public servants or black people who had achieved any kind of financial success were particular targets.

Alarmed by the violence, Congress passed the Enforcement Act in 1871, also known as the KKK Act, making it illegal to intimidate people at the polls and giving the president power to use armed forces to protect an African American's right to vote. In the end, the Klan's reign of terror died down only when the new president, Ulysses Grant (1822–1885), sent federal forces to arrest hundreds of suspected Klan members. The Klan would not re-emerge as a force until the 1920s.

But after two years of unrelenting violence and terror, many black Southerners had become afraid to exercise their voting rights. Southern governments slowly refilled with Democrats who openly ran on a "white man's party" platform.

In 1875, Senator Sumner managed to usher through another civil rights act in response to the continued civil rights violations to African Americans. The Civil Rights Act of 1875 barred racial discrimination in public accommodations and in jury service. But the Supreme Court struck it down as unconstitutional in 1883.

Although the KKK was shut down, other white supremacist groups took over.

When the presidential election of 1876 rolled around, white supremacists wanted the Democratic candidate, Samuel Tilden (1814–1886), to win rather than the Republican, Rutherford Hayes (1822–1893). The presidential race was close, and a dispute arose over 20 electoral votes. The candidate who won those votes would win the presidency. The parties disagreed so vehemently that the country teetered on the brink of civil war again. As a compromise, the Democrats agreed to concede the victory to Hayes if Hayes would withdraw federal troops from the South. Hayes agreed.

With the soldiers gone, no one was there to help African Americans exercise their right to vote. Within a year, governments in the South were nearly all-white again. They began instituting laws meant to humiliate and hurt black people. This was the start of the "Jim Crow" era.

Reconstruction was over.

POLL TAX

In 1870, the states ratified the Fifteenth Amendment to the Constitution, securing African American men's right to suffrage. But white Southerners worked around this by instituting poll taxes that blacks couldn't afford and literacy tests most couldn't pass to prohibit them from voting.

KEY QUESTIONS

- **Most Southern whites never owned slaves, yet were fiercely opposed to African American advancement or equality. Why?**

- **How might society differ today if the white supremacist backlash had not prevented African Americans from freely participating in society?**

REPARATIONS

The Oxford Dictionary defines reparations as the "action of making amends for a wrong one has done, by providing payment or other assistance to those who have been wronged." Many freedpeople believed "40 acres and a mule" would serve as reparation for the theft of their liberty and labor. But in the end, former slaves were never awarded monetary or property reparations following emancipation.

- **Research times in American or world history when reparations were made to people to compensate them for a wrong done to them.**

  - Which countries have offered reparations and to whom?

  - What kind of reparations were made?

  - What were the reparations intended to compensate the injured for?

  - What are the various benefits the reparations provided to the injured?

- **Pretend it's 1865 and you believe a reparations plan is needed for freedpeople.** What kind of proposal would you develop?

To investigate more, watch this video in which writer Ta-Nehisi Coates (1975–) presents an argument for reparations. Do you find it convincing? Why or why not?

YouTube Coates slavery reparations

Chapter 4 ▶

Separate and Unequal

IT'S NICE TO JUST DO NORMAL STUFF LIKE EAT LUNCH TOGETHER ONCE IN AWHILE.

What happened after the era of Reconstruction?

During the Jim Crow era, Southern whites constructed a society expressly designed to keep African Americans at the bottom of the social hierarchy. They did this through racist laws, extreme violence, and humiliation.

After Reconstruction ended, race relations entered one of its bleakest periods. White Southerners established a series of rigid laws and social codes of racial segregation that touched every aspect of Southern society. Although Jim Crow laws mainly targeted African Americans, many people of color battled white supremacist attitudes all across America.

One day in 1892, a man named Homer Plessy (1862–1925) bought a first-class ticket in New Orleans, Louisiana. He boarded the train and settled into a whites-only, first-class car. A conductor approached him and asked, as required by law, whether he was "colored"—meaning black. Homer answered yes. He could have said no. His great-grandmother was African, making him only one-eighth black.

The conductor asked him to move to the car for non-whites. Homer refused, saying he had a valid first-class ticket and a right to be there. The police ultimately dragged him from the train and jailed him.

Most people would never have guessed Homer's ancestry. However, like many families in New Orleans, for generations his family had identified as black Creoles—mixed race African Americans.

Homer intentionally shared his race because he was part of a test case to challenge Louisiana's Separate Car Act, which required train cars to be racially segregated. A group of Creole lawyers wanted to test the constitutionality of the Fourteenth Amendment. They believed the amendment should protect Homer's right to ride in whichever car he chose. If Homer won the case, segregated establishments all over the South would also be ruled unconstitutional.

Homer Plessy's case went all the way to the U.S. Supreme Court. In 1896, the court ruled that his constitutional rights were not violated, because, although he had to go to a separate car, the Fourteenth Amendment only protects legal, not social equality. The justices wrote, "if one race be inferior to the other socially, the Constitution . . . cannot put them upon the same plane." They concluded that because the law didn't prohibit African Americans from taking the train and the separate train cars were reasonably equal, then the Constitution hadn't been violated.[1]

The Plessy decision put the stamp of approval on the "separate but equal" way of thinking. The case marked the official start of the horrific Jim Crow era.

LIFE UNDER JIM CROW

What did life under Jim Crow mean? For African Americans, it meant living with the knowledge that certain members of society saw you as inferior and could treat you with cruelty or violence.

ONE DROP RULE

How could a man who was seven-eighths white be considered black? In that era, white society believed that even one drop of African blood sullied a person's racial purity and made them entirely black. Many light-skinned blacks, including Homer Plessy, took pride in his racial identity despite its obvious disadvantages. Others decided it was easier to "pass" as a white person and join white society. What does the one-drop rule suggest about the social construction of race?

The drinking fountain at the Halifax County Courthouse, North Carolina, in April 1938

credit: John Vachon for U.S. Farm Security Administration

ORIGINS OF JIM CROW

The name "Jim Crow" came from a minstrel performer named Thomas Rice (1808–1860). In the 1820s, he had a song-and-dance routine called "Jumping Jim Crow" in which he painted his face black, put on shabby clothes, and jumped around in a silly and degrading manner, pretending to be a slave. The act was extremely popular with white Southerners, and Jim Crow became a derogatory term for African Americans.

Every kind of public accommodation was segregated—schools, restaurants, swimming pools, water fountains, public restrooms, and even cemeteries. Signs announcing "Colored" or "White" hung over establishments to make the rules clear. In non-segregated spaces, such as stores or post offices, blacks had to wait until all whites had been served before having their turn.

Most facilities for black people reinforced their inferior status. Black schools were allowed to become dilapidated, overcrowded, and lacking in essential supplies, such as books or pencils. Train cars for "coloreds" were dirty and unheated.

STAYING IN YOUR PLACE

Jim Crow was about more than written laws. It was also about following an unwritten social code. All whites had the unwritten duty to ensure that black people "stayed in their place." African Americans were expected to never show that they thought themselves equal to whites.

It was an unwritten rule that a black person walking down the street had to step aside to allow a white person to pass. Under no circumstances could a black man touch or even make eye contact with a white woman.

Blacks couldn't call whites by their names without first attaching a title, such as "Mr." or "Miss," but whites could call African Americans whatever offensive name they wanted. A black person couldn't appear angry or offended by a white person who mistreated them—they could show only fear or submission.

> It didn't matter how much money African Americans earned, their level of education, manner of dressing or speaking—the social code applied to all.

In fact, many white people reserved particular fury for blacks who dared to seek higher education or economic success. They scornfully called such people "uppity" and tried their best to tear them down. Whites also immediately punished those black people who dared to break the social code or who were even perceived as doing so.

LYNCHING

Death at the hands of lynch mobs was the ultimate punishment for African Americans who were perceived as having violated laws or codes. Lynching is killing someone for an alleged offense without holding a trial. During the 80 years of the Jim Crow era, 3,959 black men, women, and children have been documented as murdered by lynching.

There were 15,760 legal executions in the United States from 1700 to 2017. Statistically, the Jim Crow era lynching of blacks was equivalent to 25.1 percent of 300 years of legal executions in the United States.[3]

"Strange Fruit," written in 1937 by Abel Meeropol (1903–1986), is a famous song about lynching. Listen to it below, performed by legendary singer Nina Simone (1933–2003). What poetic phrases does Abel use to convey the horrors of lynching? How does Nina use her voice to convey this message?

YouTube Simone Strange Fruit

The most common method of lynching was by hanging. White vigilantes would hear of an alleged offense—which could be as trivial as a black man bumping into or otherwise "frightening" a white woman—and a mob would storm to that person's home, drag him away, and hang him with a noose from a tree. Bodies might hang for months as a warning. Other times, blacks were killed by being burned alive, tortured, or mutilated. Their corpses were often dismembered and desecrated by the large crowds of white people who came to witness and cheer on the executions.

Few Southerners, black or white, dared to speak out against lynching, but an African American journalist named Ida B. Wells (1862–1931) was one of the brave ones. Ida became an anti-lynching activist when a friend was lynched after defending himself against a white mob attack on his store in Memphis, Tennessee.

She wrote bold anti-lynching articles in *The Free Speech and the Headlight,* a newspaper she co-owned and operated. While she was traveling in the North, a white mob destroyed her office and warned her never to return to Memphis. Ida never did, but she continued her anti-lynching crusade in the North. She later became a cofounder of the National Association for the Advancement of Colored People (NAACP).

COPING WITH RACISM

How did African Americans endure being subjected to such relentless violence, humiliation, and oppression? Many put their faith in religion. Some turned to drinking or gambling to escape feelings of despair. Others tried to work against the system as best they could.

Ida B. Wells and her children, 1909

Black people founded their own stores, banks, insurance companies, barber shops, newspapers, churches, fraternities and sororities, and clubs. Some sought higher education, despite discouragement from white society, and even sometimes their worried parents. They tried to advance their economic situation within societal boundaries.

A small minority became middle class or well-to-do, though they didn't flaunt it for fear of white punishment.

ENTREPRENEURIAL SUCCESS STORIES

In 1898, three African American men, Charles Clinton Spaulding (1874–1952), Aaron McDuffie Moore (1863–1923), and John Merrick (1859–1919), created the North Carolina Mutual Life Insurance Company in Durham, North Carolina. The company is still flourishing today with assets worth $162 million. In the early 1900s, Annie Malone (1877–1957) became the first female African American millionaire, selling hair care products for black women.

RACE REALITY

In 1910, 89 percent of black Americans lived in the South. By 1970, only 53 percent of blacks lived there. More than 6 million African Americans made the move North during this period.[4]

Most of all, African Americans learned how to present a public face that white society found acceptable. They pushed their feelings deep down and never expressed the pain, anger, or humiliation they felt in white company. This caused an identity crisis in many people as they struggled to separate their true selves and sense of self-worth from the degraded image they had to present to whites for their survival.

For many African Americans, the pressure of this existence was too much. Eventually, many black people decided to leave the South.

THE GREAT MIGRATION

Between 1916 and 1920, more than 300,000 Southern African Americans moved North, in search of both work and social and political equality. Most headed for major cities such as Chicago, Cleveland, New York, and Philadelphia. Hopes were high.

Black newspapers had touted the North as a kind of promised land. In many ways, life above the Mason-Dixon line was far better than living under Jim Crow's relentless cruelty. Black Southerners marveled at being served before a white person or entering the same door as whites. The potential for terror and death did not hang over their day-to-day existence.

However, racism was still rampant in the North. In reality, many public places were segregated. Some schools were integrated, but many weren't, and all-black schools were of inferior quality. African Americans competed for jobs with floods of European immigrants, in addition to native-born white Americans, and were typically "last hired, first fired."

Housing discrimination was also common. Many whites used racially restrictive agreements to keep blacks from renting or buying property. Under these contracts, an owner buying a new home would legally agree never to let a black person—and sometimes Asians or Jews—reside in it. Such restrictions forced African Americans to live in overcrowded, rundown urban areas.[5]

The North also had its share of racial riots.

One of the most infamous was the Chicago Riot of 1919, when a black teenager accidentally swam into the "white" part of the beach, was pelted with stones by white teens, and drowned. The police refused to arrest the perpetrators, triggering a week of rioting in Chicago between black and white gangs. Twenty-three blacks and 15 whites were killed, 537 people were injured, and more than 1,000 black families lost their homes.

By 1940, some 80 percent of properties in Los Angeles and Chicago had covenants prohibiting their use by black families.

A group of men and armed National Guard in front of the Ogden Cafe during the race riots in Chicago, Illinois, 1919

credit: Chicago History Museum, ICHi-065485; Jun Fujita, photographer

THE STRUGGLE OF RACIAL MINORITIES

EUROPEAN IMMIGRANTS

Some Europeans who immigrated to the United States in the nineteenth century also faced discrimination for their ethnicities, particularly Irish and Italians. Today, some people praise Irish and Italians for successfully assimilating into American culture and criticize some people of color for not having done the same. History tends to forget how hard and even violent assimilation can be. What are some differences between the European immigrant experience and that of people of color? How are their reasons for entering the United States significant?

African Americans may have been the most systematic targets of discrimination and racism, but they weren't the only ones. From the mid-1800s onward, both Mexicans, whether immigrants or Mexican American citizens, and Chinese immigrants suffered from widespread discrimination, violence, and lynchings. White society considered both groups racially inferior. They, too, were banned from many public spaces, such as schools and restaurants, and were squeezed into segregated ghettos.

Many Mexicans became U.S. citizens after Mexican territory, including California, Arizona, and Nevada, was acquired in the Mexican-American War in 1848. Mexican Americans and Mexican immigrants were initially welcomed and even encouraged to immigrate, as laborers were needed to develop agriculture and lay railroad tracks. Sentiment turned against them as work became scarcer.

Although the government officially classified Mexicans as "white" for decades, American white society didn't see them as such.

> Vigilante justice and lynching of Mexicans and Mexican Americans wasn't uncommon. There are 871 documented cases, but historians believe there were thousands more.[6]

Chinese immigrants streamed into the United States in the late 1840s. They fled political strife and hoped to make their fortune by laying tracks for the transcontinental railroad or mining for gold.

White society initially approved of Asians as hard workers. Animosity toward the Chinese bloomed as competition for jobs grew during the second part of the nineteenth century. Calling them the "yellow peril," whites blamed the Chinese for taking jobs and decreasing wages, and became increasingly convinced they were planning an invasion.

Eventually, the federal government deemed the Chinese a national security threat. In 1882, Congress passed the Chinese Exclusion Act, prohibiting further Chinese immigrants. Originally intended to span only a 10-year period, the ban continued for 61 years.

This was the first U.S. law to bar immigrants based on race.

Native Americans experienced a different form of racism during the late nineteenth and early twentieth centuries. Members of the federal government still believed that indigenous people could be acceptable citizens only if they would give up their culture and behave like "civilized" white Americans.

Watch a short documentary clip about the Native American boarding schools. How is watching someone's personal pain from an experience different from simply reading about the policies?

PBS education of native children

Group of Omaha boys in cadet uniforms, Carlisle Indian School, Pennsylvania, 1880

retrieved from: U.S. National Archives

Over the angry objections of their parents, the government sent thousands of Native American children to boarding school. Their sacred, long hair was chopped off, they were given Anglicized names, and they were prohibited from speaking their native languages. Army Captain Richard Pratt (1840–1924), who opened an Indian boarding school in Carlisle, Pennsylvania, saw forced assimilation as a good thing, saying famously that it would "kill the Indian in [them], and save the man."[7]

Such forced assimilation came at great cost to the Native American community. Many children suffered from extreme homesickness and abuse. Some even died from untreated diseases and during escape attempts. Those who graduated had often lost their ability to speak their indigenous languages, became isolated from their cultures, and eventually left their native communities altogether.

PATHS TO ADVANCEMENT

Despite the many obstacles they faced, people of color continued to work hard at advancing economically and socially. At the turn of the century, the black community generally had two schools of thought about how to go about this.

African American leader and former slave Booker T. Washington (1856–1915) was a champion of the "accommodation" approach. He argued that blacks shouldn't try to push for desegregation and civil rights, but should instead focus on economic self-determination within the restrictions imposed by white society. He also believed that blacks should train in the industrial arts, developing practical skills such as carpentry or farming, rather than obtain a liberal arts education.

W.E.B. Du Bois disagreed, arguing that African Americans could not achieve and maintain economic prosperity without also securing political rights.

> He believed that blacks should be classically educated and that a "talented tenth" of educated African Americans would help lead others to their full potential.

In 1905, W.E.B. Du Bois formed a civil rights group called the Niagara Movement, an organization of black professionals, then, in 1909, he became a co-founding member of the NAACP. This multi-racial organization would play a vital role in obtaining legal equality for all in the twentieth century.

In the next chapter, we'll take a look at how the NAACP and others influenced the push for civil rights that defined the 1950s and 1960s.

W.E.B. DuBois, 1911

credit: Addison N. Scurlock

VOCAB LAB

Write down what you think each word means. What root words can you find to help you? What does the context of the word tell you?

assimilation, **derogatory**, **humiliation**, **inferior**, **Jim Crow**, **lynching**, **oppression**, and **vigilante**.

Compare your definitions with those of your friends or classmates. Did you all come up with the same meanings? Turn to the text and glossary if you need help.

KEY QUESTIONS

- **Why is humiliation such an effective weapon in oppression?**

- **Do you know a family member or friend who lived during the Jim Crow period? What are their memories of this time?**

Langston Hughes, "I, Too"

🔍 Hughes I too

Claude McKay, "America"

🔍 Claude McKay America

Georgia Douglas Johnson, "When I Rise Up"

🔍 Johnson when I rise

Gwendolyn B. Bennett, "Heritage"

🔍 Afro poets heritage

Countee Cullen, "To a Brown Boy"

🔍 Countee Cullen to brown boy

To investigate more, research the rise of gospel music, jazz, and blues. Why was their development significant? How did such music impact race relations? How does music from different cultures affect race relations today?

THE HARLEM RENAISSANCE

As African Americans moved from South to North during the Great Migration of the 1900s, many black families headed to Harlem in the northern part of New York City. There, black creative, intellectual, and social life blossomed, producing an explosion of legendary writers, artists, musicians, actors, and poets. This period, which lasted from 1910 to 1930, is known today as the Harlem Renaissance.

- **Read and analyze five poems written by African American poets of the Harlem Renaissance.** Answer the following questions.

  - What are the themes of each poem?

  - What is the tone of each poem?

  - How do the poems indicate pride in black heritage or culture?

  - What joys, fears, hopes, and sorrows are revealed?

  - How do the poets feel about America?

  - What audience do you think each poem was written for?

  - Does anything about the poems surprise you?

- **Read writings from other American writers of color from this period.** Consider Jade Snow Wong (1922–2006), John Okada (1923–1971), or Zitkala-Sa (1876–1938), and reflect on the same questions.

- **Write your own poem or song.** Write from the perspective of a person of color during this period or as a white person witnessing some of the inequalities or atrocities committed.

Chapter 5 ▶
Renewing the Battle for Equal Rights

How did the civil rights movement change race relations in the 1950s and 1960s?

In the 1950s and '60s, racial tensions reached a head, as African Americans and white allies began to take a forceful stand against violence, degradation, and discrimination.

One summer evening in August 1955, a 14-year-old African American boy named Emmett Till (1941–1955) went to a store to buy some candy in rural Mississippi. Born in Chicago, Emmett was only visiting the South for the summer and he didn't understand the realities of Jim Crow. It was claimed that, as he left the store, Emmett said something mildly flirtatious to the white female cashier.

A few days later, the woman's husband and his brother showed up at Emmett's great-uncle's house. They took the boy away, ignoring the uncle's pleading. During the next few hours, they brutally beat, tortured, and mutilated the boy.

When Emmett was near death, they shot him in the head, tied a metal fan around his neck with barbed wire, and pushed him into a river. Emmett's body, battered beyond recognition, was found three days later.

When his devastated mother received his body in Chicago, she chose to have an open-casket funeral so the world could see how his murderers had brutalized her child. An African American magazine took photos of his disfigured corpse, which were quickly picked up by the mainstream media and the international press.

> People around the world reacted with horror and outrage, suddenly alert to the extreme violence against blacks in the South.

IN THE COURT

To many people, the civil rights movement seemed to spring out of nowhere in the 1950s, but the movement had been quietly growing for decades. In its earlier years, the NAACP focused on anti-lynching campaigns and equal treatment for blacks in the federal government and military with moderate success. But the organization rose to national prominence when it created the NAACP Legal Defense Fund in 1939 and sharpened its focus on desegregating public schools.

The Legal Defense Fund was headed by Charles Hamilton Houston (1895–1950), a black Harvard Law School graduate who believed that improving educational opportunities for blacks was the highest priority. Schools were segregated all over the South and black schools were still vastly inferior to white ones. Without proper education, black people could have no hope of advancement. He hired Thurgood Marshall (1908–1993), a promising African American lawyer from Baltimore, as assistant special counsel.

You can get first-hand accounts of Emmett Till's story and the Montgomery bus boycott by watching this excerpt from the documentary, *Eyes on the Prize*.

🔍 Eyes on prize part 1

RACE REALITY

Emmett's murderers were brought to trial, but were acquitted by an all-white jury within an hour. The cashier, Carolyn Bryant Donham, testified at trial that Emmett had grabbed her and used sexually lewd language. In 2017, 62 years later, she admitted that she had lied. In 2018, the U.S. Department of Justice reopened a probe into the murder.

In 1967, Thurgood Marshall became the first black U.S. Supreme Court justice.

The two African American lawyers racked up many crucial legal wins before the U.S. Supreme Court. They helped strike down the University of Maryland law school's ban on black students. They forced Texas law schools to admit African American students because the state had no equivalent school for blacks. In 1954, the Legal Defense Fund scored the biggest blow against desegregation to date with the *Brown v. Board of Education* case.

In the *Brown* case, a group of black parents filed a suit against the Kansas Board of Education. Through Thurgood and other civil rights lawyers, they argued that segregated schools violated their Fourteenth Amendment right to equal treatment and denied black students the educational opportunities that would allow their success and advancement in life.

People protesting integrated schools

credit: Library of Congress, U.S. News & World Report Magazine Photograph Collection

The case went to the Supreme Court, which unanimously ruled that racial segregation in public school was "inherently unequal." Civil rights supporters celebrated, and news of the decision was greeted with applause in all corners of the world. A year later, in a decision called *Brown II*, the Supreme Court ruled that desegregation of public schools must occur "with all deliberate speed."

THE LITTLE ROCK NINE

Many Southern communities took steps to avoid school integration. One of the most famous took place in Little Rock, Arkansas. Nine African American students, known now as "The Little Rock Nine," were scheduled to begin school at the all-white Central High on September 4, 1957. But the governor of Arkansas, Orval Faubus (1910–1994), called the Arkansas National Guard to block their entry to "preserve the peace."

The students came to school anyway.

They were supposed to meet to enter the school together, but because of a miscommunication, 15-year-old Elizabeth Eckford (1941–) ended up trying to enter the school alone. A white crowd gathered around the girl, screaming racial epithets and calling for her to be lynched as she walked toward the school, where she was barred from entering.

A judge ordered the governor to remove the National Guard, and the students were allowed to enter the school. The Little Rock Nine suffered constant abuse at the hands of their fellow students during the next several months, but eight of the nine completed the year. The next year, Governor Orval shut down all public schools until a court forced him to reopen them.

White Southerners felt their carefully constructed racial hierarchy starting to crumble. Law or not, they were adamantly opposed to desegregation and were determined to keep Jim Crow in place.

Listen to Elizabeth Eckford's experience in her own words. What surprises you about her story? How would you have reacted in her place? How do you think the people who threatened her feel about their behavior now? How might Elizabeth feel about that day now?

🔍 Elizabeth Eckford own words

NONVIOLENT RESISTANCE

Bit by bit, segregation began to erode. On February 1, 1960, four black male college students sat down at the whites-only lunch counter at a Woolworth's store in Greensboro, North Carolina, and asked to be served. They were asked to leave. They refused and continued to sit there politely until closing time. The next day, 15 black people came to sit at the lunch counter. Eventually, more than 1,000 people would crowd into the store in protest. A year later, Woolworth's desegregated the lunch counter.

The courageous act of these four young men unleashed a torrent of sit-ins and grassroots activism across the South, particularly among students in historically black universities. For the next few years, thousands of students sat in at stores and restaurants and organized mass demonstrations and protests.

The students also created formal civil rights organizations. One of the most renowned was the Student Non-Violent Coordinating Committee (SNCC), formed by a black woman named Ella Baker (1903–1986). This group took on a range of grassroots projects, from door-to-door canvassing to organizing voter registration drives for black Southerners. SNCC coordinated protests and actions with other civil rights organizations, such as the Congress of Racial Equality (CORE).

CORE was a civil rights organization that gained national attention with its "Freedom Riders" project. Freedom Riders were interracial teams who tested a 1960 Supreme Court ruling banning segregated interstate transportation by traveling on segregated buses throughout the South. They were often attacked with baseball bats, beaten, and threatened. Once, their bus was firebombed.

RACE & WORLD WAR II

Approximately 1.2 million African Americans served in World War II along with tens of thousands of Latinos, Native Americans, and Asian Americans. The war helped put America's troubled race relations in an international spotlight, as international leaders derided the United States for fighting for "freedom" while ignoring its oppression of African Americans. However, racism persisted. Two-thirds of the Japanese-American population, some 120,000 people, were forced to live in internment camps for fear that they would betray the United States. Only about 11,000 German Americans, individually selected, were so interned.

Violence against activists was sometimes state-sanctioned. In Alabama, Eugene "Bull" Conner (1897–1973), the commissioner for public safety, regularly turned fire hoses and attack dogs on peaceful protestors. In 1965, on a day now known as "Bloody Sunday," Alabama state troopers teargassed and violently clubbed hundreds of African Americans and whites as they, led by Martin Luther King Jr., peacefully marched from Selma to Montgomery, Alabama, for voting rights. In all these cases, no matter how badly the marchers were abused, they did not fight back.

Not all African Americans supported nonviolence at all costs, however. Malcolm X (1925–1965) was a popular African American leader who believed that black people were in the midst of a revolution, and that if whites were not willing to give blacks the vote and equality, then it would be morally acceptable for blacks to use violence to achieve their goals. As support for his views, he cited the American, French, and Russian Revolutions.

DR. MARTIN LUTHER KING JR.

African Americans had several leaders in this era, but none was as prominent and revered as Martin Luther King Jr. (1929–1968). The minister from Atlanta, Georgia, had charisma, authority, and moral certitude that transcended race and class. He believed that nonviolence "offered one of the most potent weapons available to oppressed people in their struggle for freedom." Why do you think nonviolence was such a key weapon?

The March to Selma, 1965

credit: Abernathy Family

CIVIL RIGHTS LEGISLATION

In the spring of 1963, President John F. Kennedy (1917–1963) drafted a civil rights bill, but was assassinated before the bill could become law. The task fell to his successor, Lyndon B. Johnson (1908–1973).

President Johnson was a Democrat from Texas who supported both civil rights and the eradication of poverty. He was able to use his relationships with other Southern politicians to pass the Civil Rights Act of 1964. This act banned segregation on the grounds of race, religion, or national origin in all public places, and barred employers and labor unions from discriminating on those grounds as well.

A year later, Johnson shepherded the Voting Rights Act of 1965 through Congress. It outlawed discriminatory voting practices, such as poll taxes, literacy tests, and other administrative restrictions that had been used since post-Reconstruction to prohibit or discourage African Americans from voting.

Three years later, Congress passed the Fair Housing Act, also known as the Civil Rights Act of 1968, which prohibited discrimination against people in the sale or rental of houses based on race, color, religion, sex, disability, familial status, or national origin. But these acts could not erase more than 300 years of racist thinking and discrimination.

BLACK POWER

By the mid-1960s, the United States was bitterly divided, not just over racial issues, but over the U.S. involvement in the Vietnam War and other social issues. Groups whose views had been long suppressed—people of color, women, youth—were now finding their voices and speaking out.

DEATH OF BOYS

The KKK was in full swing in the 1960s, spreading terror and death all over the South. Michael Schwerner (1939–1964) and Andrew Goodman (1943–1964), who were white, and James Chaney (1943–1964), who was black, fatally attracted the Klan's attention while in Mississippi registering black voters. Klansmen kidnapped, shot, killed, and buried the three activists in an unmarked grave. The state of Mississippi refused to prosecute the alleged murderers, though seven were convicted in federal court.

Black identity was also shifting. Many African Americans began rejecting the term "Negro" and preferring the term "black." They began to preach black economic independence and embraced their African ancestry.

As they continued to face beatings and aggression during protests, a growing number of blacks were beginning to question whether nonviolence was the right way to go. In addition, tensions between African Americans and police in poverty-stricken black neighborhoods led to a series of violent and destructive riots in big cities across America. Millions of dollars in property were destroyed and 23 people were killed.

Clashes with the police and concerns of police brutality led to the founding of black militant groups, such as the Black Panther Party, which supported fighting back against the police in self-defense.

> The riots, along with the rise of black militancy, frightened white society.

Some claimed the riots were proof of the lawless and violent nature of African Americans rather than the expression of pent-up anger and frustration after centuries of abuse.

PEOPLE OF COLOR

African Americans were not alone in their struggle for equality. Latinos, Asian Americans, and Native Americans repeatedly fought against segregation and unequal educational opportunities throughout the first half of the twentieth century. They became more active during the 1960s.

THE KERNER COMMISSION

President Johnson appointed an 11-person committee known as the Kerner Commission to investigate the cause of the riots and offer recommendations. After seven months of investigation, the committee concluded that "white racism" and discrimination were the underlying causes of the unrest. It emphasized that police brutality alienated the black community. After the report's release, 53 percent of white Americans polled condemned the report for implicating white behavior in the riots. The report recommended that state governments, among other things, take steps to create new jobs, dilute the ghettos by ensuring that black people had access to different types of housing, and hire a more diverse police force.

Cesar Chavez speaking at a rally in 1974

James Baldwin (1924–1987) was a highly eloquent African American writer of novels and essays. Read his 1966 essay, "Occupied Territory," describing the realities of police brutality in poor black neighborhoods. What themes and situations are still relevant today?

 Nation Baldwin occupied

In 1962, Cesar Chavez (1927–1993) and Dolores Huerta (1930–) founded the United Farm Workers to fight the exploitation of migrant farm workers. With Filipino activists, they successfully led the nation's first major grape boycott, demanding better wages and work conditions for grape pickers. Millions of people stopped eating grapes, and the boycott was a huge success. Other boycotts and strikes brought attention to workers' rights in the 1970s.

The Asian American community, which often faced hostility from the public during the Vietnam War, came together as a single racial group and became more outspoken about its concerns about oppression and discrimination. Many began objecting to being called "Orientals," which labeled them as outsiders—instead, they preferred to be called Asian Americans.

During this period, Japanese Americans began fighting for reparations to compensate them for their internment during World War II. President Ronald Reagan (1911–2004) eventually awarded them reparations some 20 years later.

In the 1960s, Native Americans grew more forceful in defending their rights. Tribal leaders made legal challenges to protect the remainder of their land, citing treaty violations, and won several important victories. In 1968, four Native Americans formed the American Indian Movement (AIM) to help destitute Native Americans in cities and to push for more government funding toward Native American-controlled organizations.

In a symbolic victory, AIM took over and occupied Alcatraz Island in San Francisco Bay in 1969, claiming that their occupation should establish American Indian rights to the land. The federal government removed them from the island in 1971.

SAY GOODBYE

On April 4, 1968, Martin Luther King Jr. went to Memphis, Tennessee, to speak in support of a strike of sanitation workers. After delivering his famous "mountain top" speech on a hotel balcony, a white man called James Earl Ray (1928–1998) shot and killed the minister. Upon the news of the murder, more than 1,000 riots broke out all across America, as African Americans erupted in fury and grief. More than 35 people died during the next few days, and cities such as Chicago and Washington, DC, burned.

The death of Martin Luther King Jr. is usually considered the end of the civil rights movement, but it was only the end of widespread public protests and marches. For the next two decades, civil rights advocates pushed for schools and businesses to adhere to the civil rights legislation that had been put in place. But, as overt racism diminished and African Americans could not decide upon a united way forward, white support for civil rights policies began to wane.

RACE REALITY

In large cities such as New York City and Indianapolis, Indiana, disturbances after Martin Luther King Jr.'s murder were minimal. Most historians believe this was because political figures in those cities went directly into the black community immediately after the assassination to offer sympathy and understanding. Why might that have made a difference?

KEY QUESTIONS

- How did the media influence the civil rights movement?

- Would you risk your life for any political, religious, or social cause? Why or why not?

- Do you think white society's attitudes toward the 1960s riots were hypocritical? Why or why not?

THE IMPORTANCE OF THE VOTE

Voting is a fundamental part of a democracy. African Americans, Latino Americans, Native Americans, Asian Americans, and women have had to fight to obtain the right to vote in the United States. The Voting Rights Act of 1965 was enacted to secure those rights.

Inquire & Investigate

VOCAB LAB 📖

Write down what you think each word means. What root words can you find to help you? What does the context of the word tell you?

boycott, **integration**, **internment camp**, **nonviolence**, **poll tax**, **riot**, and **segregation**.

Compare your definitions with those of your friends or classmates. Did you all come up with the same meanings? Turn to the text and glossary if you need help.

- **Read the text of the original Voting Rights Act of 1965.** What was the impact on people of color? How about in your state? How many registered voters were there in each racial group in the years preceding 1965? In the years after?

- **Even today, there are still issues of whether state actions are unfairly inhibiting or preventing certain Americans from exercising their right to vote.** Some of these issues include: a) gerrymandering; b) voter purging; c) voter suppression; d) access to the ballot; and e) felony disenfranchisement.

- **Divide into groups of five and prepare a presentation on each of these issues, one per group.** Explain the issue, describe the people it affects, discuss the seriousness and pervasiveness of this issue, and discuss what (if anything) is being done to address the issue.

> **To investigate more,** research the Supreme Court's 2012 ruling that struck down a key provision of the Voting Rights Act. What was the provision about? Why was it struck down? Has the striking of the provision affected voting rights? If so, how? What other parts of the Voting Rights Act might soon be reviewed by the Supreme Court? Why?

Chapter 6 ▶
A Color-Blind Society?

IS IT POSSIBLE TO ESCAPE OUR PAST?

What happened after the civil rights movement?

During the presidency of Lyndon B. Johnson, his administration implemented many programs meant to help the poor, people of color, and women achieve equality. But within a decade of President Johnson's "Great Society" programs, politicians began weakening or dismantling them.

After the upheaval of the 1960s, race relations proceeded in relative peace through the next few decades. But as explicit acts of racism and violence against African Americans diminished, some began using less obvious, though still highly damaging, means of resisting government efforts to level the playing field for those historically discriminated against in employment and education.

Affirmative action originated in 1961 when President John F. Kennedy issued an executive order creating the Committee on Equal Employment Opportunity. Federal contractors were mandated to "take affirmative action to ensure that applicants are employed, and that employees are treated during employment, without regard to their race, creed, color, or national origin." After the passage of the Civil Rights Act of 1964, Kennedy's successor, President Johnson, issued a similar executive order and, two years later, included women.

The intent behind affirmative action was to help racial minorities and women gain greater access to jobs and educational institutions. Employers or college admissions officers were mandated or encouraged either to give preference to people of color or women or to set aside a certain percentage of positions for them.

Coupled with civil rights laws banning discrimination, affirmative action helped bring significant social and economic advances for African Americans. In the late 1960s and 1970s, black enrollment in colleges doubled, the rate of black unemployment dwindled, and the gap between white and black employment began to narrow.

Many whites, however, saw affirmative action as unfair. They argued that the policy allowed for less-qualified minorities to take educational and employment positions at the expense of whites who were more qualified. Many argued that an individual's ability and skill level should be the standard for hiring someone or admitting them to a school, and that taking race into account was "reverse discrimination."

Read the transcript of President Johnson's speech at Howard University in which he explained the rationale behind affirmative action. How do you think the students felt hearing this speech? How about opponents of affirmative action?

🔍 presidency Johnson 301

In 1961, Vivian Malone became the first African American student at the University of Alabama.

credit: Warren K. Leffler, U.S. News & World Report Magazine

Allan Bakke didn't discuss the 36 white students with lower grades than him who had also been admitted to the medical school, or that the university also reserved five spaces for children of alumni and faculty and university sponsors, some of whom also had lower scores than him.

CODED LANGUAGE

Following the civil rights movement, politicians almost never mentioned race in a derogatory way but instead used coded language to refer to race. For example, because African Americans were disproportionally represented among the U.S. poor and tended to live in urban areas, the term "inner city" became a coded way to say "poor black people." In this way, politicians could accurately say they never referred to race, even while getting a racially charged message across.

Supporters of affirmative action countered that because whites had such enormous educational, economic, and social advantages, any race-neutral admissions process or hiring policy would only continue to give whites an unfair advantage. Affirmative action, however, could reduce these inequalities by bringing more minorities into the workforce and schools until the educational and economic gaps were significantly reduced.

The issue came to a head in the mid-1970s, when a white man named Allan Bakke (1940–) sued the University of California at Davis medical school for reverse discrimination after being denied admission. Allan argued that because the medical school had reserved 16 of its 100 slots for educationally and economically disadvantaged minority students, and some of those minorities had lower grades and test scores than him, he had been discriminated against because of his race.

In 1978, the Supreme Court ruled that racial quotas such as those used at the University of California were unconstitutional. It noted that universities could take race into consideration to increase the diversity of the student body, rather than to remedy historical discrimination. By the mid-1980s, the rate of minority enrollment in universities began to decline sharply, but the Bakke decision wasn't the only reason.

A COLOR-BLIND SOCIETY

In the 1960s, President Johnson established several social programs designed to help improve the economic circumstances of impoverished Americans. Among these were financial grants for college students, expanded Social Security, and help to establish the Job Corps, which provided work and vocational training resources.

The programs were barely underway before some people began pushing back against them. Some objected to federal funds being used to assist the poor because this increased the federal budget. Others insisted that these programs encouraged the poor to abuse or rely on the federal system.

> Presidential candidate Ronald Reagan, running on a campaign of welfare reform, helped enhance perceptions of abuse.

During a 1976 campaign rally, he described a woman living the high life with hundreds of thousands of stolen welfare funds as if she was the norm. While some people did exploit the system, Reagan's "welfare queen" was not representative of the majority of Americans receiving government assistance. However, that didn't stop many from unfairly using the example of the welfare queen as a symbol for all people on government assistance. Although Reagan never mentioned the woman's race, public assistance and welfare abuse quickly became synonymous with being African American.

When Ronald Reagan became president in 1980, the administration immediately began slashing the funding for programs that assisted the poor, including funding for higher education grants and nutritional programs for children. The administration also eliminated the public service employment program and reduced benefits for the working poor.

About 70 percent of Reagan's federal budget cuts came from programs affecting the poor.[1] These cuts were devastating for poor people, but especially African Americans and Latinos, who were disproportionally represented among the poor.

African American homeownership rose by nearly 6 percent during the three decades following the passage of the Fair Housing Act of 1968.[2]

THE ORIGINAL WELFARE QUEEN

The woman President Reagan referred to in his speech was Linda Taylor (1926–2002), a racially ambiguous woman who was listed as "white" in a 1930 census, though she sometimes presented herself as black, Native American, Asian, or Jewish. She was a con artist of extreme proportions. In addition to cheating the government, she was a bigamist, stole from private individuals, misrepresented herself as a nurse and doctor, and was suspected of kidnapping and murder.

With less financial aid available, black enrollment in college dropped from 34 percent to 26 percent. Thousands of African Americans in the public service employment program lost their jobs. By 1989, the black unemployment rate was more than twice that of whites, leaving them slightly worse off than 10 years earlier, when the unemployment rate was *only* twice that of whites.[4]

THE WAR ON DRUGS

As budget cuts affecting the poor occurred throughout the 1980s, the cocaine drug scourge hit America. Cocaine is a dangerous, highly addictive, and illegal drug. In the 1980s, a cheaper, smokable form of cocaine, known as crack, was developed.

A 1989 government drug trafficking report emphasized that "drug abuse was evident, if not the norm, in widely varying geographic and demographic settings." In fact, another government report estimated that 80 percent of U.S. cocaine users were "middle-class white suburbanites." In the 1980s and '90s, cocaine was especially associated with affluent Wall Street investment bankers.

Crack was more prevalent in poor African American communities. Moreover, many young black teens, trapped in poor quality schools and discouraged by sky-high unemployment rates, began selling crack to earn money. Deadly gang wars erupted in major U.S. cities, and the homicide rate among black youth ages 14 to 17 more than doubled between 1984 and 1994.[6]

Many saw the problem as a public health issue. In contrast, the Reagan administration launched a "War on Drugs" that criminalized both drug users and sellers.

The administration funneled billions into the budgets of federal law enforcement agencies to combat the illegal drug trade. At the same time, it sharply decreased funding for drug treatment, prevention, and education.

To make matters worse, in 1986, Congress passed the Anti-Drug Abuse Act, which established mandatory minimum sentences for specific quantities of cocaine. But the sentencing ratios were wildly imbalanced. Drug dealers caught selling 5 grams of crack would receive a five-year minimum federal prison sentence, but a cocaine dealer would only receive the same sentence if caught selling 500 grams of cocaine. Lawmakers justified this 100:1 sentencing disparity because they argued that crack was much more addictive than cocaine. (The ratio was lowered 18:1 in 2010.)

The nationwide prison population exploded, going from 350,000 in 1972 to more than 2 million in 2010. Numerous studies have shown that blacks, whites, and Latinos use and sell drugs at very similar rates. Yet African Americans are arrested on drug charges at five times the rate of whites.

Drug-related crimes accounted for the majority of the increase in prison populations, as did harsh sentencing laws that led to lengthier sentences served. African Americans soon made up 45 percent of the prison population, even though they are only 13 percent of the U.S. population. Latinos were also disproportionally imprisoned.

Given the similar use of drug rates and disproportionate imprisonment rates, many researchers believe the discrepancy is because of racial bias against African Americans and Latinos. Some say this bias has led the police to target black and brown men based solely on their skin color.

COLOR-BLIND

On the first national observance of Martin Luther King Jr.'s birthday, President Reagan gave a national radio address in which he rejected racial quotas, citing the civil rights leader's goal of a color-blind society. Read that speech below. Compare it to Martin Luther King Jr.'s speech, also below. Do you think Martin Luther King Jr. would have agreed with President Reagan's use of color-blindness? Why or why not?

🔍 ucsb Reagan MLK radio speech • Yale MLK dream

RACE REALITY

Numerous studies have shown that blacks, whites, and Latinos use and sell drugs at very similar rates. Yet African Americans are arrested on drug charges at five times the rate of whites.

> **Some studies suggest that people may have a skewed perception of different racial groups because of the way races are portrayed in the news and the media.**

This bias is at the root of racial profiling, a practice where police stop, question, and search people based primarily on their race. Starting in the mid-1980s, the police began stopping tens of thousands of African American and Latino male drivers to search their cars for drugs. Drivers were—and continue to be—stopped on any pretext, such as broken taillights or failing to use their turn signals. Their cars were searched even when the offense didn't warrant it.

Proponents of the practice argue that blacks and Latinos were targeted more often because they were arrested more often for having drugs. But critics pointed out that such reasoning was circular. If the police primarily focus on black and brown people, it follows that they'd be more likely to find drugs among that group, while drug-carrying whites went undetected.

People protesting racial profiling

credit: longislandwins (CC BY 2.0)

THE BLACK MIDDLE CLASS

Even as many African Americans remained caught in a cycle of poverty, under-education, and imprisonment in the 1980s, the black middle class was slowly growing. With schools making greater efforts to diversify their campuses and classrooms, the number of black lawyers, doctors, and other professionals increased. The number of black-owned small businesses grew between 1982 and 1987, with earnings reaching more than $20 billion.

African Americans also became more visible in popular culture and the media. Although stereotyped images of blacks as poor or criminals persisted, in the mid-1980s, America fell in love with an empathetic talk show host named Oprah Winfrey (1954–). Basketball star Michael Jordan (1963–) became not just a sports legend, but also a successful brand. African Americans became more prominent in politics, too, with dozens of congressional representatives and a few senators.

Interpersonal race relations generally improved. The number of interracial marriages climbed. By 2013, more than 87 percent of Americans approved of interracial unions. This is a sharp change from 40 years earlier, when interracial marriage was still illegal in 19 states and fewer than 20 percent of Americans approved.[6]

Given all the race-related bloodshed, upheaval, and grief that occurred in the centuries before, the relative peace of the late twentieth and early twenty-first centuries gave many the impression that American race relations had turned a corner. Many people of color continued to experience racism and unequal treatment in their daily lives, but these issues only rarely spurred widespread protests or discussion. After the election of President Obama, however, some of these grievances began to rise to the surface.

RACE REALITY

Latinos, Native Americans, and especially Asian Americans also saw a growing middle class in the late twentieth century, but experienced relatively little visibility in popular culture or the media beyond stereotypical images. Can you think of any examples of stereotypical images in books, movies, or television?

KEY QUESTIONS

- Can American society ever be truly color-blind? Should it be? Why or why not?

- Do you think grades and test scores should be the sole criteria for admissions into schools? If so, why? If not, what other factors do you think should come into play? Why?

PERCEPTION VS. REALITY

What is the racial composition of America's poor? Drug users? College graduates? Criminals? Millionaires? Your perceptions may not accurately match reality. To stay aware of what's what with respect to racial composition in America, look at official statistics.

 census historical poverty

 samhsa survey drug use

 bjs correctional population

- **Test yourself!** Write down your estimates of the racial composition of whites, African Americans, Latinos, Asian Americans, and Native Americans. Then, review official data to check your answers. These links will get you started.

- **In the United States, what is the racial composition** of the general population, the middle class, millionaires, the prison population, people who receive welfare or public assistance, people who use illegal drugs, and college graduates?

- **Create a bar chart of your estimates and the results for each category and racial group.** In which categories were you most accurate? Least? Why? What statistic surprised you the most?

> To investigate more, compare the opioid and heroin crises of the late-2010s with the crack cocaine epidemic of the 1980s. How were these similar? How were they different?

Chapter 7 ▶
The Post-Racial Illusion

What did it mean for a black man to be elected president of the United States?

The Obama era saw the rise of a new social justice movement, a white nationalist movement, and increasingly heated discussions of race-related issues.

President Obama's historic win in 2008 gave the impression to some that America's race-related problems would soon be a distant memory. But even as Obama's election showed how far American race relations had evolved, the years that followed revealed just how far it still has to go.

When President Obama took office in 2009, he knew racism wasn't dead. He'd faced it on the campaign trail as his opponents implied that he was dishonest and that his loyalties didn't lie with the United States. Images of his face photoshopped with a monkey's muzzle circulated the internet. A conspiracy theory swirled that he was born in Kenya, not Hawaii, spurring him to produce his birth certificate mid-presidency. In numerous instances, Obama figures were lynched in effigy and hung from trees.

But President Obama rarely commented publicly on the racist vitriol against him. He once remarked, "If I stopped to think about it, I'd be paralyzed."

President Obama shaking hands with the next generation in November 2012

credit: Pete Souza, White House photographer

In fact, some African Americans criticized President Obama for speaking so rarely on racial issues while in office. But, as a growing number of sensitive racial issues took center stage in 2012, he could not avoid the topic.

TRAYVON MARTIN

One of the issues that did prompt President Obama to speak out about race involved the killing of a black teenager. On February 25, 2012, a 17-year-old high school student named Trayvon Martin (1995–2012) bought candy and ice tea from a convenience store in Sanford, Florida. He left the store and headed toward his father's girlfriend's house, where he was staying. An hour later, Trayvon was dead. He was shot by George Zimmerman (1983–), a 28-year-old man who self-identifies as a white Hispanic, who was volunteering for a neighborhood watch.

Watch Obama's speech below and read one white person's reaction to it. Do you think Obama's speech was appropriate? Why do you think he chose to approach the issue this way? With respect to the reaction, do you agree with the author? What are the most and least convincing parts of this article? Why?

YouTube Obama Trayvon Martin • National Review Trayvon Martin

George Zimmerman claimed that Trayvon attacked him and that he shot Trayvon in self-defense. Because Trayvon died at the scene, his side of the story is unknown. It is known, however, that a 911 dispatcher advised George to stop following Trayvon, but George continued to do so. It's also known that Trayvon told his girlfriend by phone that a "creepy" white man was following him. A recording also indicated that there was an argument and a scuffle before George fired the shot. George was arrested for the shooting and charged with second-degree murder nearly two months after the shooting.

African Americans were overwhelmingly horrified. Hearing painful echoes of Emmett Till's fateful trip to the store, many felt that George targeted Trayvon because he was a black male rather than because of any particular suspicious behavior. A Reuters/Ipsos poll showed that 91 percent of black Americans felt the shooting was unjustified—but only 35 percent of whites felt similarly.[1]

Eventually, George was tried in court for second-degree murder and manslaughter. In 2013, a six-person jury found him not guilty, and he went free. The African American community was devastated.

> For many, it was yet another moment in American history where a white person took a black life without suffering legal consequences.

Just after the verdict, an African American woman named Alicia Garza (1981–) wrote a Facebook post about her sadness over the verdict and her compassion for the pain the black community felt. She ended the post with the words: "Black people. I love you. I love us. Our lives matter."

Her friend, Patrisse Cullors (1984–), touched by the post, added the hashtag #blacklivesmatter. From these posts sprang a new social justice movement.

BLACK LIVES MATTER

The Black Lives Matter movement began simply. Alicia Garza, Patrisse Cullors, and their friend Opal Tometi (1984–) set up social media accounts urging people to share why they believed black lives mattered. Later, they led a protest in California with signs and posters saying "Black Lives Matter."

The movement gained national attention in August 2014 after Ferguson, Missouri, erupted in anger and violence. A grand jury had decided not to indict a white policeman who had fatally shot an unarmed 18-year-old black man named Michael Brown (1996– 2014).

Alicia and her friends immediately organized "freedom rides" to Ferguson to protest the killing. Protesters marched through the streets chanting "Black Lives Matter."

An activist holds a "Black Lives Matter" sign at a protest following the officer-involved shooting of Jamar Clark on November 15, 2015, in Minneapolis.

credit: Tony Webster (CC BY 2.0)

COULD HAVE BEEN ME

The outcry and divisiveness over the verdict in the Trayvon Martin case led Obama to make a statement about it. He spoke in a personal way, saying, "Trayvon could have been me 35 years ago," and urged non-black Americans to understand how painful the case was for African Americans, considering their long history of discrimination. His speech received both praise and disparagement from white Americans. Many people argued that discussing his personal feelings was unpresidential and inflated racial tensions.

Although the majority of Black Lives Matter events have been peaceful, people have criticized the group for several incidents where some protest participants behaved aggressively or shouted inflammatory language during protests or speeches.

The chant spread across the nation. When they returned home, the friends began establishing the Black Lives Matter Global Network.

The organization's purpose is to end state-sanctioned violence against black people, help fight for police accountability, and promote other forms of social justice through demonstrations, civil disobedience, and community outreach. Its website states it welcomes people of all races and sexuality to participate in the movement, and are unapologetically "black and queer affirming."

Soon, a backlash formed against the movement. Many white conservatives found the name and concept of the organization "anti-white" or "anti-police." Some even compared the group to the KKK.

Clamor against the organization grew louder in 2015, when a black Army veteran shot five white military officers in Dallas, Texas, saying he wanted revenge for police killing black men. Although he was not associated with Black Lives Matter, and the organization forcefully denounced his actions, many people blamed the organization anyway.

Some people began using the term "All Lives Matter" in response to the Black Lives Matter slogan.

Proponents argued that whites would be more sympathetic to the cause if the name were more inclusive. Black Lives Matter members and supporters countered that the organization's name is not trying to say that *only* black lives matter, but that black lives, which have not been highly valued throughout American history, matter as much as other lives.

POLICE BRUTALITY

As the Black Lives Matter movement got underway, the deaths of unarmed African Americans at the hands of U.S. policemen became increasingly publicized. Often captured on video by police body cameras, scenes of violence against black males went viral on social media. African Americans were outraged to witness these deaths, some of which occurred when no crime was being committed. Black Lives Matter protests swelled in response.

A 2015 *Washington Post* study, which tracked fatal police shootings in real time, showed that although whites make up 69 percent of the population, they comprise 49 percent of those killed by police. African Americans make up 13 percent of the population but are 24 percent of those fatally wounded.

This means that blacks are 2.5 times more likely than whites to be killed by police.[2]

Some people argued that African Americans are disproportionately more likely to commit violent crimes, relative to their population. Other statistics from the Mapping Police Violence project show that police are more likely to use force on blacks and people of color even when they are unarmed or otherwise posing no threat. The statistics also show that 34 percent of blacks killed by police in 2017 were unarmed and not "attacking."[3]

Others remarked that it was hypocritical for blacks to protest police killings of African Americans, when far more black people died at the hands of other blacks.[4] However, studies indicate that everyone is more likely to die at the hands of someone of their own race.

CAUGHT ON CAMERA

Around 2012, police departments across the country began using body cameras and dashboard cameras to monitor police interactions with the public. As a result, the public witnessed numerous killings of African Americans where the victim posed no threat to the police or public. Twelve-year-old Tamir Rice (2002–2014) was shot by the police while playing with a toy gun in his neighborhood. Philando Castile (1983–2016) was shot while reaching for his wallet to show his identification after a policeman pulled him over for having a broken taillight. Why might seeing such incidents make African Americans feel a particular sense of outrage and injustice?

The more African Americans and others protested police brutality and the more some white people insisted that there was no problem, the more strained race relations became. Race relations became even more inflamed when, in 2016, Colin Kaepernick (1987–), an NFL quarterback, refused to stand for the national anthem in protest of the police brutality against African Americans.

Many people were incensed, finding his actions disrespectful to the flag, veterans, and country. But Colin continued his protest, later kneeling during the anthem along with some of his teammates. The protest did receive some support from some teams and players, a few coaches and owners, and many members of the public. But society at large did not support it. In 2017, Colin was released from his contract and has not played for the NFL since.

RISING WHITE ANXIETY

Numerous African American organizations and societies seek to help reduce crime, improve education, offer mentorship opportunities and training, boost employment rates, and fix other societal conditions that give rise to crime in black communities. Why might these organizations attract less attention than protests?

As the debates over police brutality continued, signs were growing that working-class white Americans were caught in the grip of a crisis. In 2015, a study revealed that the death rate among middle-aged, working-class whites was rising due to alcohol abuse, suicide, and drug overdoses of prescription opioids and heroin. By 2018, whites in this demographic were 50 percent more likely to die of a drug overdose than African Americans and 167 percent more likely than Latinos.[5]

Some social scientists theorize that this increase in drug abuse and death rates is due to the white working class's despair over the lack of stable, blue-collar job opportunities. Many have been unable to improve their financial situation.

In addition, some whites were beginning to feel anxious about the changing demographics of the United States. Whites have been the majority racial group in the United States since the country's founding, but now projections show that whites could be a minority by 2045. Some small towns are seeing this change unfold before their eyes.

For example, Hazleton, Pennsylvania, once a town with a clear white majority, is now majority Latino. Some white residents say that although they live together peaceably in the community, they feel "outnumbered."

#MAGA

In June 2015, wealthy businessman and reality television personality Donald Trump (1946–) announced that he would run as a Republican candidate for president. He promised to "drain the swamp" of the political establishment and institute tax and other reforms to help the working class.

> At first, the media and other presidential candidates didn't take him seriously, as he frequently spoke and behaved in a manner that many considered outside the bounds of respectability.

But running under the slogan "Make America Great Again," candidate Trump found a strong following among many working-class, white Americans. Some believed he sincerely wanted to help those who felt forgotten by the Democratic Party. His rhetoric appealed to many people who felt that he "tells it like it is" and that he echoed their own feelings.

STATUE STATUTES

America experienced additional racial divisiveness in 2017 over the issue of taking down statues in the South of Confederate Army soldiers from the Civil War. Many people felt that because the statues glorified people who supported white supremacy and racial oppression, they should be removed. Others felt that removing them was like revising or masking history. What is your opinion? Why?

The Brookings Institute forecasts that by 2045, whites will comprise 49.9 percent of the population, Latinos 24.6 percent, African Americans 13.1 percent, Asians 7.8 percent, and multiracial people 3.8 percent.[6] Such projected changes have led some white people to feel worried about being left behind.

Some people feel that "Make America Great Again" is an example of dog-whistle politics. Do you agree? Why or why not?

Other Americans were appalled by Donald Trump's characterization of Mexican immigrants as criminals and rapists, and felt his proposed Muslim ban unfairly cast suspicion on all Muslims as terrorists. Two days after a black activist was shoved and kicked by white supporters during a Trump rally, the candidate tweeted grossly inaccurate statistics about black-on-white crime.

Many felt that the presidential candidate promoted an atmosphere of hate and intolerance, especially when several white supremacist and far-right groups spoke out in support of him. Among these was David Duke (1950–), formerly a prominent leader in the KKK. Nonetheless, in November 2016, Donald Trump was elected president of the United States.

GROWTH OF HATE CRIMES

As racial tensions rose, so did reported hate crimes. In 2015, 5,818 hate crimes were reported, a 6.8-percent increase from the previous year. In 2016, the number grew by 6 percent, and in 2017, it increased by 12 percent in the country's 10 largest cities. African Americans were the most targeted group, but crimes against Muslims, Jews, and Latinos also increased significantly.[8]

In 2015, a self-identified white supremacist entered an African American church in Charleston, South Carolina, during a Bible study meeting and sprayed the all-black group with bullets as they closed their eyes to pray, killing nine. In 2017, a white man stabbed an African American college student to death days before the young man was to graduate. That same year, during a white nationalist "Unite the Right" rally in Charlottesville, Virginia, a white supremacist plowed into a crowd of protesters with his car, killing a young white woman.

On social media and the internet, numerous people reported stories of being targets of hate and even captured some of the incidents on video. Asian Americans spoke of being told to "go back to China." In more than one state, white classmates taunted Latino schoolchildren with chants of "Build the wall!" On two occasions, nooses were found in the National Museum of African American History and Culture in Washington, DC.

Debates over Latino immigration and President Trump's ban of people from certain Muslim countries created further uproar and division. Many people argued that the Trump administration's zero-tolerance policy for Latinos perceived to be unlawfully entering or living in the United States was racist and dehumanizing, especially the aspect of the policy that separated children from their parents at the U.S. border. Others argued that it was necessary to stem the tide of migrants entering the country illegally.

One arguably positive effect from all the strife, however, is that the realities of race have again become a topic of national conversation. The question is: Where do we go from here?

WHITE-ON-WHITE CRIME

According to the Southern Poverty Law Center, it's a common misconception that African Americans are responsible for the majority of murders of white people. FBI statistics have consistently shown that most homicides are committed within racial groups. For example, 2015 FBI statistics show that 82 percent of whites killed were killed by other whites, while 90 percent of blacks killed were killed by other blacks.

KEY QUESTIONS

- Is there a difference between having "white pride" and "black pride" or "Native American pride" or "Irish pride"? If so, what are the differences?

- What role has the internet played in bringing attention to race-related issues? Has it played a positive role, a negative role, or both?

- Presidents Obama and Trump have both been blamed for deteriorating race relations. How can a president set the tone for race relations?

START A MOVEMENT

Young adults have been responsible for initiating numerous important social movements throughout American history. How do they go about it?

- **Research and analyze a specific social movement in American history.** In your analysis consider the following.

  - What were the goals of the movement?
  - Who was part of the movement?
  - What were the main methods of bringing attention to this particular issue?
  - What slogan was used? Why?
  - What legal arguments were used to support the movement's position? What moral ones?
  - How did it use the mainstream media or social media to spread its message?
  - What made the protest effective (or not)?

- **Select an important issue that you'd like to bring to the attention of your school, community, or the public.** Using all the information you learned from the movement you just researched, develop a written plan for your own movement.

> **To investigate more,** choose an influential leader or group of leaders of an American social movement in history and research how that person or persons were viewed by society at the start of their movement. How are they viewed now? Is it possible to effectively protest a sensitive issue without upsetting the status quo? Why or why not?

VOCAB LAB 📖

Write down what you think each word means. What root words can you find to help you? What does the context of the word tell you?

backlash, **brutality**, **civil disobedience**, **demographics**, **hate crime**, **injustice**, and **intolerance**.

Compare your definitions with those of your friends or classmates. Did you all come up with the same meanings? Turn to the text and glossary if you need help.

Chapter 8 ▶
Continuing the Good Fight

How do we continue to improve race relations in America and around the world?

It may feel uncomfortable to discuss race relations, but having open yet civil conversations about race is key to working through the country's racial problems.

American society has come a long way since the days of slavery and overt racism. Yet widespread racial inequality, harmful biases, and discrimination (and sometimes violence) against people of color continue to persist. The good news is that many people of all colors are engaging in the conversations we need to have to understand each other better, recognize racially biased behavior, and improve American race relations in a genuine and enduring way.

For most of American history, racism and discrimination have been easy to recognize. Racism was explicitly written into laws. Even when it wasn't, society expressed and maintained a clear racial hierarchy through obvious discriminatory behavior.

Thankfully, such overt racist behavior occurs much less frequently now than it did before the 1970s. A difficult side effect of having less explicit racism, however, is that discrimination and bias have become much harder to identify.

This has led many people to falsely believe that racial prejudice is no longer a widespread problem or that it has little negative effect on people of color. But there is much evidence to the contrary.

RECOGNIZING THE PROBLEM

Numerous studies in the twenty-first century have revealed the existence of damaging biases against people of color. This is especially true for African Americans and Latinos in employment, housing, education, and more.

For example, in 2004, two economists conducted a study where they sent out thousands of identical résumés to employers. The only difference in the résumés was the names of the applicants. Half the résumés used names the scientists expected job recruiters to associate with white applicants, while the other half used names that recruiters were expected to read as belonging to black applicants. They found that people with names recruiters could assume belonged to white applicants were twice as likely to be called for an interview.[1]

Studies have shown that such racial biases can start as early as preschool and kindergarten. Black preschoolers are 3.6 times more likely than whites to receive out-of-school suspensions. Does this mean that black preschoolers are actually causing more problems? Not according to studies.

In 2016, Yale University researchers conducted a study in which teachers were asked to watch a video of four young children, a black boy and girl and a white boy and girl, interacting in a classroom. The teachers were asked to look for signs that the children were presenting challenging behavior.

THE MODEL MINORITY

Some Asian Americans feel excluded from the national discussion of racial discrimination and bias because American society has held them up as a "model minority." The economic and educational success of many Asian Americans is seen as proof that hard work and discipline can triumph over racial discrimination. But some Asian Americans reject this label, pointing out that it puts massive pressure on Asian American students. Some also argue that it's used to create a racial wedge and doesn't consider the differences in the Asian American experience relative to that of other people of color. Others note that certain Asian American groups continue to struggle economically and that Asian Americans still face plenty of bias, discrimination, and stereotyping.

The video showed no challenging behavior. Nonetheless, 42 percent of the teachers said the black boy was presenting challenging behavior.[2]

The Brookings Institute found that in interracial school fights, black children receive longer punishments than white children. Another study found that African American men were featured in 70 percent of televised crime news reports in Omaha, Nebraska, during a three-month period, although they represented only 31 percent of arrests made during that period. What could explain these numbers?

UNCONSCIOUS BIAS

Social scientists say these discrepancies reveal an unconscious or implicit bias against black people or people of color. This means that many people in positions of power—employers, teachers, media heads—sometimes hold prejudices against people of color and discriminate against them without even realizing it or intending to do so.

Such unconscious discrimination can have numerous negative ripple effects on people of color. Bias in employment hiring makes it more difficult for people of color to find jobs. Bias in schools can alienate and discourage children of color from learning. Seeing an overrepresentation of images in the media of African Americans as criminals or Latinos as undocumented immigrants can lead to inaccurate and exaggerated perceptions of blacks or Latinos as lawbreakers.

These negative perceptions of people of color can contribute to higher unemployment rates, increased school dropout rates, and feelings of alienation and hopelessness. The unfortunate consequences, in turn, can enhance stereotypical perceptions of those racial groups, starting the cycle all over again.

The College of Du Page's Latin American Studies Committee hosts a salsa/merengue/Bachata dance to introduce participants to the dance and music of Latin America. Why are events such as this important?

credit: COD Newsroom (CC BY 2.0)

EVERYDAY RACISM

Countless people of color in America report experiencing bias in their everyday lives. Many of these experiences aren't instances of overt or violent racism, but consist of comments, actions, and subtle aggressions rooted in racial stereotypes and bias.

This is sometimes called "everyday racism."

While people of color have spoken of their experiences with bias and discrimination for ages, only recently have others been able to see how such experiences play out in real life. The prevalence of cell phones has allowed many people of color to capture some of their experiences on video and share them widely on social media.

In 2018, numerous videos and stories about white people calling the police on African Americans and other people of color went viral, including the following instances.

- A Starbucks employee called the police because two African American men, who were waiting for a friend, were sitting in Starbucks without ordering anything.

- A white woman called the police on African Americans because they were having a barbecue in a park in Oakland, California.

- A white man called the police on an African American woman because she was enjoying a community swimming pool in her residential development and wouldn't show him her ID.

- A white woman called the police on an 8-year-old African American girl because she was selling water outside her apartment building without a permit.

- A white woman called the police on two Native American brothers on a college campus tour because their appearance "made her nervous."

- A white woman called the police on a black student because the person was napping in a common room in a dorm at Yale University.

- A white person called the police to report a black woman who had rented an Airbnb apartment, because the caller assumed the black woman had broken in.

- Golf course employees called the police about a group of black women because they believed they were playing golf too slowly.

- A neighbor called the police on a black state legislator who was conducting a door-to-door campaign.

Some say that standing up for others who are being treated unfairly will make the difference in race relations. These two videos show ordinary people taking a stand against acts of racial bias. Why might such acts help?

🔍 Vox arrested Starbucks
• Univision Latina Muslim harassment

Many sociologists and people of color believe these incidents indicate that some white Americans view public spaces as theirs to control and protect from anyone they judge does not belong there.

This realization leaves many people of color feeling both frustrated and angry that, even after hundreds of years, the struggle to be seen as and treated as equal to whites continues.

MICROAGGRESSIONS

Another common form of everyday racism is called microaggression. Racial microaggressions are comments, gestures, or actions that, intentionally or unintentionally, communicate an insulting, belittling, or hostile message to people of color based on race.

For example, when people lock their car doors as an African American or Latino person walks by, or when African Americans are trailed by security officers in a store, those acts are considered microaggressions. They tell the person of color they are seen as untrustworthy. Many Asian Americans born and raised in the United States experience it as a microaggression when they are complimented on their English or asked, "Where are you *really* from?" This implies they're seen as perpetual foreigners.

Native Americans experience it as a microaggression when they are greeted with "Hau" or are called "Chief" or some other stereotypical name. People of color are also commonly told by white friends that they don't see them as black/Asian/Latino/Native American. Why might a comment such as this be considered a microaggression?

Some sociologists note that white people have been policing black people for ordinary, nonthreatening behavior since the slavery era. The difference is that now people of color can stand up for themselves and call attention to these incidents through social media.

RACE REALITY

Microaggressions can occur against a range of marginalized groups, from women to those with physical limitations to those in the LGBTQ community.

While microaggressions might seem like minor annoyances to people who have never faced them, they can be very frustrating and hurtful to those who experience them repeatedly. Microaggressions occur far more frequently than people outside a particular racial group realize, and can occur in countless subtle ways—sometimes even being conveyed by a certain tone of voice, facial expression, or other body language.

The subtlety of these small aggressions can leave many people of color frustrated as they try to assess how the comment, gesture, or action was intended, compare it to previous incidents, and decide whether and how to respond. The accumulation of these tiny slights and insults and the effort required to decide how to handle the situation can lead to feelings of exhaustion, offense, and anger. These feelings are compounded when the experiences are ignored or minimized by society.

WHITE PRIVILEGE

The flip side of discussions of racial bias and microaggression is the concept of white privilege, or the advantages that white people have in American society due to their skin color. For example, white people have the privilege of shopping, driving a car, or enjoying a public space without worrying that someone will assume they have criminal intent or don't belong because of their skin color.

Most white Americans also have the reassurance of almost always being around people who look like them, especially in positions of authority. When moving to a new neighborhood or new school, most white people have the privilege of not worrying that their neighbors or fellow students will be unfriendly because of their skin color.

We all have privileges in different ways, though some people, of any race, can have more than others. Watch this video for a visual representation of how privilege can operate. Where might you end up on the privilege scale?

🔎 YouTube what is privilege

A person at a Black Lives Matter protest, 2014

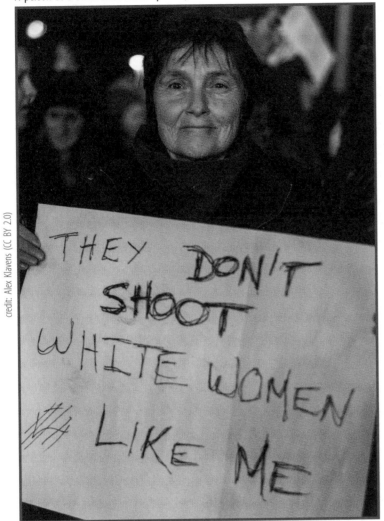

THEY DON'T SHOOT WHITE WOMEN LIKE ME

RACE REALITY

Some people find the term "white privilege" offensive, believing it implies that all white people are wealthy or guaranteed an easy life. Others think it's code for calling someone racist or used to silence people or make them feel guilty. However, the phrase "white privilege" is not meant to suggest that white people don't ever struggle, can't be poor, or are all racist. It is simply meant to indicate the absence of certain struggles, obstacles, and challenges in the lives of white people that people of color face solely due to the color of their skin. Although the phrase can be misused at times, asking someone to "check his/her privilege" is meant to encourage someone to consider how their privileges as a white person may be influencing their opinion of a particular situation.

An individual white person's bad judgment, crimes, or mistakes are not attributed to the character of their entire race. Nor does society congratulate high-achieving whites as being a "credit" to their race. Privileges such as these mean most white people live in society without thinking much about their race at all.

They also lead white people to wonder why people of color can't do the same.

HOPE FOR THE FUTURE

Watch lifelong interracial friends discuss their friendships on video. What were some of the benefits? Some of the challenges? How can interracial friendships reduce prejudice?

🔍 interracial BFFs talk

Most Americans today do not have a favorable view of the state of race relations. In August 2018, 55 percent of those polled by Politico/Morning Consult said they believe race relations have worsened since November 2016. Of those who felt this way, 79 percent were African American, 60 were Latino, and 51 percent were white. Sixteen percent of those polled said race relations have improved, and 18 percent said there has been no change.

What will finally make a difference in improving race relations?

Some say that change will come when people examine their attitudes, admit to their racial biases, and consciously work to overcome them. Others say that race relations will improve when people stop focusing on or talking about race.

Many professionals who study race relations say that our best hope lies with educating children. Studies show that when children work together in racially diversified classrooms and groups, they are less likely to display racial bias. Others show that interracial friendships and relationships reduce prejudice.

Many people hope that by helping children to become more familiar with the different experiences and realities of Americans of all colors, as adults they'll reject racial biases. They will be less likely to perpetuate stereotypes about racial groups. This will help bring about a more genuinely inclusive and equal society that truly lives up to the honorable ideals expressed at America's founding.

KEY QUESTIONS

- **What do you think will help improve race relations? Why?**

- **Is understanding historical context important in discussions about race relations? Why or why not?**

- **What actions can you take personally to help improve race relations in your life or community?**

MOVING BEYOND STEREOTYPES

The best way to resist stereotyping other racial groups is by developing genuine friendships with people from other races and getting to know their lives and cultures firsthand. You can also learn by reading blogs, books, and magazine articles, watching films, and visiting museums.

- **Explore the culture of a racial group different from your own by taking virtual visits of museums and centers dedicated to specific racial groups.** Use the links on page 116 to get started.

- **Keep a "stereotype journal" for three days.** Each time you see, hear, or read an example of a stereotype on television, in the news, in social media, or in your personal life, make a note. What groups are stereotyped most often? What common stereotypes did you observe?

- **Keep an "anti-stereotype" journal for three days.** Find persons, characters, or images that reject racial stereotyping. Note the source and the form of the anti-stereotype. What groups aren't often stereotyped? What groups aren't much represented at all?

To investigate more, watch the eight mini-films collectively titled "A Conversation On Race" on *The New York Times* website. What do some of the stories have in common? What different opinions did you notice *within* racial groups? Across racial groups? What surprised you?

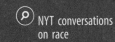 NYT conversations on race

GLOSSARY

abolish: to end something.

abolitionist: a person who supported ending slavery.

accountability: the state of being obligated to accept responsibility for a certain thing or action.

activism: the policy or action of using strong campaigning to bring about political or social change.

activist: a person who works for social or political change.

adaptation: a change that a living thing makes to become better suited to its environment.

affirmative action: a policy or practice that seeks to improve employment and education opportunities for people who have been historically discriminated against.

agriculture: growing plants and raising animals for food and other products.

ally: united for a common goal.

amnesty: a government pardon for a person who has committed a crime.

ancestor: a person from your family or culture who lived before you.

Anglicize: to make English in form or character.

animosity: hostility.

assimilation: the process of changing one's culture to be absorbed into a new culture.

backlash: a strong negative reaction.

belittling: dismissive of a person or thing.

bias: a tendency to see things a certain way, perhaps unreasonably or unfairly.

biological: relating to life and living processes.

Black Codes: a series of laws imposed in the South after the Civil War that tried to force blacks back into plantation work.

blacklist: a list of persons considered untrustworthy, suspicious, disfavored, or to be avoided.

bondage: in captivity.

boycott: to refuse to use a certain service or purchase goods in protest.

breed: to produce babies.

brutality: great physical and mental cruelty.

carpetbagger: Northerners who went south after the Civil War to profit from Reconstruction or to help carry out the federal government's plans.

categorize: to put things into different groups based on their characteristics.

catastrophic: extremely harmful or damaging.

certitude: absolute certainty.

characteristic: a feature of a person, such as blue eyes or curly hair.

charisma: compelling charm.

chattel: movable property.

citizenship: legally belonging to a country and having the rights and protection of that country.

city-state: an independent state that consists of a city and its surrounding territory.

civil disobedience: the refusal to observe certain unjust laws as a form of peaceful political protest.

civil rights: the basic rights that all citizens of a society are supposed to have, such as the right to vote.

civil rights era: a nationwide movement for racial equality in the United States during the 1950s and 1960s.

Civil War: the war in the United States, from 1861 to 1865, between the states in the North and the slave-owning states in the South.

civility: formal politeness and courtesy.

civilization: a community of people that is advanced in art, science, and government.

classification: to systematically arrange items into groups based on common features these items have.

climate: the weather patterns in an area during a long period of time. Also the general situation or attitudes that people have at a particular time.

cocaine: a highly addictive drug extracted from coca leaves.

colonist: a settler living in a new land.

colony: a country or area that is under the partial or full political control of another country.

collaborator: a person who works jointly on a project or works traitorously with an enemy.

compromise: to resolve a problem by each side agreeing to giving up some demands.

Confederate: refers to the group of Southern slave states that seceded from the Union and formed their own government in 1861.

confiscate: to take property.

connotation: an idea or feeling suggested by or associated with a word.

contemporary: modern, existing now, belonging to the current moment.

contempt: a feeling that someone or something is unimportant and deserves no respect.

cotton gin: a machine that separates the seeds from raw cotton fibers.

covenant: an agreement.

crack: hard form of the addictive drug, cocaine.

Creole: people of mixed European and African descent.

culture: the customary beliefs, social forms, and institutions of a particular people or society.

curtail: to reduce.

debt: a sum of money that is owed.

dehumanize: to treat someone or make someone feel as if they weren't human.

demographics: statistical data about a particular human population.

derogatory: unkind actions or words intended to express a low opinion of someone.

desecrate: to treat with violent disrespect.

desegregation: the process of ending segregation of people according to racial, religious, or other differences.

destitute: extremely poor.

discrepancy: a lack of compatibility between two or more facts.

discrimination: treating people unfairly because of certain characteristics, such as their gender, race, religion, or sexual orientation.

disenfranchisement: to deny someone the right to vote.

displace: to force people, animals, or things from their usual place.

disproportionate: something that is too large or too small compared with something else.

diversity: a variety of people from different backgrounds.

domestic: relating to a person's home or country.

dominate: to exercise power or control over.

dysentery: an intestinal infection resulting in diarrhea.

economy: a country's or region's production and consumption of goods and services.

emancipation: being set free from the control of something.

emigrate: to leave one's own country in order to settle in another country.

empathetic: the ability to understand and share in the feelings of another person.

enslave: to make someone a slave.

epithet: an abusive word or phrase.

equality: being treated the same, with the same rights and opportunities as others.

eradicate: to eliminate completely.

ethnicity: relating to a group of people who share a common national, racial, or religious background.

GLOSSARY

euphoria: a feeling of intense excitement.

evict: to force someone from a property.

evolution: the gradual change of living things during thousands of years.

explicit: very clear.

exploit: to benefit unfairly or unkindly to one's own advantage at the expense of someone else.

export: a good sent to another country for sale.

felony: a very serious crime.

freedom dues: payment made to indentured servants once they finished their terms of service.

Freedom Riders: people who challenged racial laws in the American South during in the 1960s.

fugitive: someone who escapes or runs away.

gender: the behavioral, cultural, or psychological traits typically associated with masculinity and femininity.

genetics: the study of genes and heredity. Genes are basic units in our cells that carry characteristics from one generation to the next.

genocide: the intentional mass killing of a race, ethnicity, or cultural group.

gerrymandering: manipulating the boundaries of voting districts to benefit a particular political party.

ghetto: a section of a city inhabited by one minority group.

grassroots: regular people seeking to make a political, social, or economic change from the ground up.

Great Migration: the movement of millions of African Americans from the South to the North, Midwest, and West between 1916 and 1970.

grievance: a complaint.

harassment: aggressive pressure or intimidation.

harmonious: different things that blend together agreeably.

hate crime: a crime motivated by racial, sexual, or other prejudice, typically involving violence.

hereditary: something determined by genetic factors that may be passed from parent to child.

heritage: the cultural traditions and history of a group of people.

hierarchy: a system of people or things that are ranked or divided according to levels.

humiliation: the act of injuring someone's dignity and making them feel foolish and ashamed.

hypocrisy: saying you believe in certain actions or principles, but behaving in a way that doesn't follow those beliefs.

identity: the unique characteristics of a person, country, or group.

immigrate: to come to a new country to live there permanently.

immoral: something that goes against what is generally accepted as moral, or right.

implication: a conclusion that can be drawn from something not explicitly stated.

implicit bias: unconscious biases, expectations, or tendencies in an individual.

impoverished: the state of being extremely poor.

incarcerate: to imprison.

incite: to encourage or stir up.

incompatibility: the inability for two things different in nature to exist at the same time.

inconsistency: the relation between two things that cannot both be true at the same time.

inequality: differences in opportunity and treatment based on social, ethnic, racial, or economic qualities.

indentured servant: a person under contract to work for a person for a certain period of time in exchange for food, shelter, and transportation.

indigenous: native to a land.

GLOSSARY

inferior: lower in rank or status or quality.

inflammatory: speech that arouses violent feelings.

ingrained: deeply embedded and therefore difficult to remove.

inhumane: cruel, heartless.

iniquitous: wicked.

injustice: something that is very unfair or unequal.

integration: bringing people of different races together.

intellectual: requiring the use of the intellect or rational mind.

internalize: to make certain attitudes, beliefs, or behavior part of one's nature.

internalized racism: the personal conscious or subconscious acceptance of the dominant society's racist views.

international: involving two or more countries.

internment camp: a prison or detention camp used during wartime.

interracial: existing between different races.

intimidation: the act of making another person fearful with threats or other shows of power.

intolerance: the unwillingness to accept views, beliefs, or behavior that differ from one's own.

Jim Crow: the practice of discriminating against African Americans through legal enforcement and social sanctions in the South in the United States, from the late eighteenth century into the twentieth century.

jubilant: feeling great happiness and triumph.

justice: fair treatment under the law.

Ku Klux Klan (KKK): a terrorist group formed after the Civil War that believes white Christians should hold the power in society. It uses violence against African Americans and other minority groups.

Latino: a person of Latin American origin living in the United States.

legacy: the lasting influence of a person or thing through generations.

LGBTQ: lesbian, gay, bisexual, transgender, queer.

liberty: freedom, the ability to act or live freely as one chooses.

literacy: the ability to read and write.

lynching: to punish a person without legal authority, usually by hanging.

mandate: an authoritative command or instruction.

mandatory: required.

Manifest Destiny: the nineteenth-century belief that God intended white Americans to expand across North America.

melanin: a pigment occurring in the hair, skin, and eyes of people and animals.

microaggression: a comment or action of a person of a dominant group that subtly reveals a prejudice or reinforces a stereotype of a person in a non-dominant group.

Middle Ages: the period of European history from the fifth century to the fifteenth century.

migrant: a person who moves from one place to another to find better living or work conditions.

militant: combative and aggressive in support of a political or social cause.

militia: civilians who band together to act in a military-like fashion.

minority: a part of the population that is different or is a smaller group.

moral: relating to right and wrong behavior and character.

motivation: a reason to do something.

NAACP: the National Association for the Advancement of Colored People, a group formed in the early twentieth century to advance justice for African Americans.

narrative: a story or account of events.

nonviolence: characterized by not using physical force or power.

GLOSSARY

norm: something that's normal or usual.

nuance: a slight difference that may be difficult to notice but is fairly important.

oppression: an unjust or cruel exercise of authority and power.

optimism: hope and confidence about the future or how something will work out.

overt racism: racism that is intentional and usually very recognizable.

paternalism: when the government or another authority tries to completely control a certain population, supposedly for the benefit of that population.

pejorative: expressing contempt or disapproval.

perception: a particular way of understanding or thinking about something.

permeate: to spread throughout something.

pigmentation: the coloration of living tissue by pigment.

poll: the process of voting in an election or to record the opinion of people on an issue.

poll tax: a payment to the government that was sometimes required before allowing a person the right to vote.

post-racial: when racial prejudice and discrimination no longer exist.

prejudice: a preconceived opinion or judgment about someone that is not based on reason or actual experience.

premature: early.

privilege: a right or benefit that is given to some people but not to others.

procreation: having babies.

proponent: a person who supports a theory, proposal, or action.

Quaker: a member of the Religious Society of Friends, a Christian movement devoted to peaceful principles.

queer: an inclusive term used to identify with the LGBTQ community as a whole. It may also relate to a gender or sexual orientation that does not correspond with established ideas about sexuality and gender.

quota: a limit on the number of people or objects.

race: a group of people of common ancestry who share certain physical characteristics such as skin color.

race relations: relations between members or communities of different races within one country.

racial: relating to race.

racial profiling: the use of race or ethnicity as grounds for suspecting someone of having committed a crime.

racism: the belief that some races are superior to others and have the right to dominate them.

racist: describes the hatred of people of a different race.

radical: someone who favors extreme social, political, or economic reform.

rancorously: characterized by bitterness or resentment.

ratify: to officially approve something.

rebel: to fight against authority or a person who fights against authority.

rebellion: an act of open or violent resistance.

Reconstruction: the period of time after the Civil War when the United States was reorganized and reunited.

reparation: to make up for a past wrong.

resistance: to fight to prevent something from happening.

reverse discrimination: discrimination against a majority group in favor of a historically discriminated-against minority group.

rhetoric: speaking or writing that intends to persuade.

riot: a gathering of people protesting something, which gets out of control and violent.

savage: fierce, uncontrolled, and ferocious.

scalawag: a post-Civil War white Southerner who supported the federal government during Reconstruction.

secede: to formally withdraw from membership of a federal union.

segregated: to be separated, often among racial, ethnic, or religious lines.

segregation: the practice of keeping racial, ethnic, or social groups separate.

sensibility: a sensitivity that makes one likely to be offended by a particular action.

sit-in: a form of protest where the protestors occupy a place and refuse to leave until their demands are met.

slave: a person considered the legal property of another and forced to work without pay, against their will.

slavery: when slaves are used as workers.

slum: a dirty and overcrowded place where very poor people live.

social: living in groups.

social construct: an idea that has been created and accepted by the people in a society.

social injustice: when people are treated unequally within a society.

social scientist: a person who studies human society and societal relationships.

society: an organized community of people.

sociologist: a person who studies human social behavior.

status quo: the current state of things.

stereotype: a judgment made without sufficient evidence about a group of individuals or the inaccurate belief that all people who share a single physical or cultural trait are the same.

sub-Saharan: describes the part of Africa that is south of the Sahara Desert.

subjugate: to repress someone.

submission: obeying or yielding to the will of someone else.

subordinate: of secondary importance.

suffrage: the right to vote in political elections.

superiority: the state of being superior to or better than something else.

supremacy: the position of being accepted or established as superior to all others in some field or activity.

systemic racism: the policies and practices that are a part of established institutions that harm certain racial groups and help others.

trade: the buying, selling, or exchange of goods and services between countries.

traffic: to buy or sell illegal goods or illegally move people.

trajectory: the path of something.

transatlantic slave trade: the buying and selling of enslaved Africans to buyers in Europe and the Americas that lasted from the fifteenth through the nineteenth centuries.

transcend: to move beyond the limits of something.

treaty: a formal agreement between two parties relating to peace, trade, and/or property.

tribe: a large group of people with the same language, customs, and beliefs.

unconstitutional: not in accordance with the laws or rules of the U.S. Constitution.

uncultivated: land that has not been prepared for growing crops.

Underground Railroad: a secret network of routes and safe houses used by abolitionists to guide runaway slaves to freedom.

Union: the United States, but especially the Northern states during the American Civil War.

uprising: an act of resistance or rebellion against a person or group in charge.

vagrancy: having no permanent home or means of making a living.

vehemently: forcefully, with energy.

vigilant: to stay alert to potential problems.

vigilante: someone who takes the law into their own hands to punish lawbreakers.

vitriol: harsh criticism.

white supremacy: the racist belief that white people are superior to those of all other races, and should therefore dominate society.

RESOURCES

BOOKS

Anderson, Carol. *We Are Not Yet Equal: Understanding Our Racial Divide*. Bloomsbury YA, 2018.

Fremon, David K. *The Jim Crow Laws and Racism*. Enslow Publishers, 2000.

Horton, James Oliver, and Horton, Lois E. *Slavery and the Making of America*. Oxford University Press, 2005.

Kendi, Ibram X. *Stamped From the Beginning: The Definitive History of Racist Ideas in America*. Nation Books, 2016.

Mettger, Zak. *Reconstruction: America After the Civil War*. Dutton. New York, New York, 1994.

Dunbar-Ortiz, Roxanne. *An Indigenous People's History of the United States*. Beacon Press, 2015.

Weatherford, Carole Boston. *The African-American Struggle for Legal Equality*. Enslow Publishers, 2000.

Ziff, Marsha. *Reconstruction Following the Civil War*. Enslow Publishers, 1999.

MUSEUMS AND WEBSITES

Amistad Research Center: amistadresearchcenter.org

Museum of Chinese in America: mocanyc.org

Smithsonian Asian Pacific American Center: smithsonianapa.org

Smithsonian Latino Center: latino.si.edu

Smithsonian National Museum of African American History & Culture: nmaahc.si.edu

PAGE 109 QR CODES

 National Museum of African American History and Culture

 American Latino Museum

 Smithsonian Asian Pacific American Center

 National Museum of the American Indian

QR CODE GLOSSARY

page 5: youtube.com/watch?v=_r4c2NT4naQ

page 7: learner.org/series/biographyofamerica/prog10/feature/index.html

page 21: nationalhumanitiescenter.org/pds/maai/emancipation/text1/buyingfreedom.pdf

page 23: poemhunter.com/phillis-wheatley/poems

page 24: web.csulb.edu/~jlawler/Course%20DW/VirginiaSlaveLaws.htm

page 29: loc.gov/exhibits/declara/ruffdrft.html

page 33: ualrexhibits.org/tribalwriters/artifacts/Family-Stories-Trail-of-Tears.html

page 37: docsouth.unc.edu/neh/tgm.html

page 42: freedmen.umd.edu/sfo15.htm

page 48: law.nyu.edu/sites/default/files/civilrightsactspeeches.pdf

page 50: youtube.com/watch?v=eB1S9-GsBW8

QR CODE GLOSSARY (CONTINUED)

page 56: youtube.com/watch?v=ughAVo2ZAag

page 58: xroads.virginia.edu/~HYPER/DUBOIS/ch01.html

page 61: pbs.org/video/american-experience-us-governments-education-native-american-children

page 64: poetryfoundation.org/poems/47558/i-too

page 64: poets.org/poetsorg/poem/america-2

page 64: poets.org/poetsorg/poem/when-i-rise

page 64: afropoets.net/gwendolynbennett5.html

page 64: genius.com/Countee-cullen-to-a-brown-boy-annotated

page 67: youtube.com/watch?v=Ts10IVzUDVw

page 69: facinghistory.org/resource-library/her-own-words-elizabeth-eckford

page 74: thenation.com/article/report-occupied-territory

page 79: online.hillsdale.edu/document.doc?id=286

page 83: presidency.ucsb.edu/documents/radio-address-the-nation-martin-luther-king-jr-and-black-americans

page 83: avalon.law.yale.edu/20th_century/mlk01.asp

page 86: census.gov/data/tables/time-series/demo/income-poverty/historical-poverty-people.html

page 86: samhsa.gov/data/sites/default/files/NSDUHresultsPDFWHTML2013/Web/NSDUHresults2013.pdf

page 86: bjs.gov/index.cfm?tid=11&ty=tp

page 90: youtube.com/watch?v=MHBdZWbncXI

page 90: nationalreview.com/2013/07/white-persons-reaction-obamas-trayvon-martin-speech-lee-habeeb

page 92: independent.co.uk/news/world/americas/black-lives-matter-awarded-sydney-peace-prize-a7759031.html

page 104: univision.com/univision-news/united-states/hispanic-woman-defends-muslim-indian-passengers-on-new-york-city-subway-being-harassed-by-another-latina

page 104: vox.com/identities/2018/4/14/17238494/what-happened-at-starbucks-black-men-arrested-philadelphia

page 106: youtube.com/watch?v=hD5f8GuNuGQ

page 108: youtube.com/watch?v=CqBYdT4jJHI

page 109: nytimes.com/interactive/projects/your-stories/conversations-on-race

page 116: census.gov/data/tables/time-series/demo/income-poverty/historical-poverty-people.html

page 116: americanlatinomuseum.org

page 116: smithsonianapa.org

page 116: americanindian.si.edu

SOURCE NOTES

INTRODUCTION

1 news.gallup.com/poll/111817/americans-see-obama-election-race-relations-milestone.aspx

2 edition.cnn.com/2017/08/16/politics/blacks-white-racism-united-states-polls/index.html

CHAPTER 1

1 Jordon, Winthrop D. *White Over Black: American Attitudes Toward the Negro, 1550–1812.* W.W. Norton & Co. Inc., 1968, p. 4–7.

CHAPTER 2

1 masshist.org/publications/adams-papers/view?id=ADMS-04-01-02-0107

2 loc.gov/exhibits/jefferson/159.html

3 userpages.umbc.edu/~bouton/History407/SlaveStats.htm

4 archives.gov/education/lessons/blacks-civil-war

RESOURCES

SOURCE NOTES (CONTINUED)

CHAPTER 3

1 Foner, Eric. *Reconstruction: America's Unfinished Revolution 1863–1877*, Harper & Row, 1988, p. 78.

2 Foner, Eric. *Reconstruction: America's Unfinished Revolution 1863–1877*, Harper & Row, 1988, p. 104.

3 docsouth.unc.edu/fpn/leigh/leigh.html

5 Oshinsky, David. *Worse Than Slavery*. Free Press, 1996, p. 273.

6 spartacus-educational.com/USAjohnsonA.htm

CHAPTER 4

1 law.cornell.edu/supremecourt/text/163/537

2 Litwack, Leon F. "Trouble in Mind: Black Southerners in the Age of Jim Crow." Knopf, 1998, p.333.

3 time.com/82375/every-execution-in-u-s-history-in-a-single-chart

4 census.gov/dataviz/visualizations/020

5 bostonfairhousing.org/timeline/1920s1948-Restrictive-Covenants.html

6 history.com/news/the-brutal-history-of-anti-latino-discrimination-in-america

7 historymatters.gmu.edu/d/4929/

CHAPTER 6

1 library.cqpress.com/cqresearcher/document.php?id=cqresrre1984030900. Congressional Quarterly, Inc. Budgeting for America, 1982, p. 99.

2 www2.census.gov/library/publications/1992/demographics/sb92-06.pdf

3 thenation.com/article/exclusive-lee-atwaters-infamous-1981-interview-southern-strategy

4 census.gov/prod/cen1990/wepeople/we-1.pdf

5 Anderson, Carol. *White Rage: The Unspoken Truth of our Racial Divide*. Bloomsbury, 2016, p. 131.

6 news.gallup.com/vault/212717/gallup-vault-americans-slow-back-interracial-marriage.aspx intellectualtakeout.org/article/gallup-poll-interracial-marriage-reveals-stunning-shift-public-opinion

7 pnas.org/content/114/39/10324

CHAPTER 7

1 articles.latimes.com/2012/apr/13/nation/la-na-nn-trayvon-martin-gun-rights-poll-20120413

2 washingtonpost.com/national/study-finds-police-fatally-shoot-unarmed-black-men-at-disproportionate-rates/2016/04/06/e494563e-fa74-11e5-80e4-c381214de1a3_story.html?utm_term=.948534117869

3 policeviolencereport.org

4 cbsnews.com/news/giuliani-blacks-crime-problem-dallas-police-rap-music-chicago

5 acsh.org/news/2018/04/05/white-overdose-deaths-50-higher-blacks-167-higher-hispanics-12804

6 brookings.edu/blog/the-avenue/2018/03/14/the-us-will-become-minority-white-in-2045-census-projects

7 nationalgeographic.com/magazine/2018/04/race-rising-anxiety-white-america

8 ucr.fbi.gov/hate-crime/2016/topic-pages/victims

CHAPTER 8

1 nber.org/digest/sep03/w9873.html

2 theguardian.com/world/2016/oct/04/black-students-teachers-implicit-racial-bias-preschool-study

INDEX

INDEX